permanent subjugation, whether made by Assyrians, Persians, Greeks, Parthians, or Turks, and remains to this day as independent of the great powers in its neighborhood as it was when the Assyrian armies first penetrated its recesses. Nature seems to have constructed it to be a nursery of hardy and vigorous men, a stumbling-block to conquerors, a thorn in the side of every powerful empire which arises in this part of the great eastern continent.

The northern mountain country—known to modern geographers as Eiburz—is a tract of far less importance. It is not composed, like Zagros, of a number of parallel chains, but consists of a single lofty ridge, furrowed by ravines and valleys, from which spurs are thrown out, running in general at right angles to its axis. Its width is comparatively slight; and instead of giving birth to numerous large rivers, it forms only a small number of insignificant streams, often dry in summer, which have short courses, being soon absorbed either by the Caspian or the Desert. Its most striking feature is the snowy peak of Demavend, which impends over Teheran, and appears to be the highest summit in the part of Asia west of the Himalayas.

The elevated plateau which stretches from the foot of those two mountain regions to the south and east is, for the most part, a flat sandy desert, incapable of sustaining more than a sparse and scanty population. The northern and western portions are, however, less arid than the east and south, being watered to some distance by the streams that descend from Zagros and Elburz, and deriving fertility also from the spring rains. Some of the rivers which flow from Zagros on this side are large and strong. One, the Kizil-Uzen, reaches the Caspian. Another, the Zenderud, fertilizes a large district near Isfahan. A third, the Bendamir, flows by Persepolis and terminates in a sheet of water of some size—lake Bakhtigan. A tract thus intervenes between the mountain regions and the desert which, though it cannot be called fertile, is fairly productive, and can support a large settled population. This forms the chief portion of the region which the ancients called Media, as being the country inhabited by the race on whose history we are about to enter.

Media, however, included, besides this, another tract of considerable size and importance. At the north-western angle of the region above described, in the corner whence the two great chains branch out to the south and to the east, is a tract composed almost entirely of mountains, which the Greeks called Atropatene, and which is now known as Azerbijan. This district lies further to the north than the rest of Media, being in the same parallels with the lower part of the Caspian Sea. It comprises the entire basin of Lake Urumiyeh, together with the country intervening between that basin and the high mountain chain which curves round the south-western corner of the Caspian, It is a region generally somewhat sterile, but containing a certain quantity of very, fertile territory, more particularly in the Urumiyeh basin, and towards the mouth of the river Araxes.

The boundaries of Media are given somewhat differently by different writers, and no doubt they actually varied at different periods; but the variations were not great, and the natural limits, on three sides at any rate, may be laid down with tolerable precision. Towards the north the boundary was at first the mountain chain closing in on that side the Urumiyeh basin, after which it seems to have been held that the true limit was the Araxes, to its entrance on the low country, and then the mountain chain west and south of the Caspian. Westward, the line of demarcation may be best regarded as, towards the south, running along the centre of the Zagros region; and, above this, as formed by that continuation of the Zagros chain which separates the Urumiyeh from the Van basin. Eastward, the boundary was marked by the spur from the Elburz, across which lay the pass known as the Pylse Caspise, and below this by the great salt desert, whose western limit is nearly in the same longitude. Towards the south there was no marked line or natural boundary; and it is difficult to say with any exactness how much of the great plateau belonged to Media and how much to Persia. Having regard, however, to the situation of Hamadan, which, as the capital, should have been tolerably central, and to the general account which historians and geographers give of the size of Media, we may place the southern limit with much probability about the line of the thirty-second parallel, which is nearly the present boundary between Irak and Fars.

The shape of Media has been called a square; but it is rather a long parallelogram, whose two principal sides face respectively the north-east and the south-west, while the ends or shorter sides front to the south-east and to the northwest. Its length in its greater direction is about 600 miles, and its width about 250 miles. It must thus contain nearly 150,000 square miles, an area considerably larger than that of Assyria and Chaldaea put together, and quite sufficient to constitute a state of the first class, even according to the ideas of modern Europe. It is nearly one-fifth more than the area of the British Islands, and half as much again as that of Prussia, or of peninsular Italy. It equals three fourths of France, or three fifths of Germany. It has, moreover, the great advantage of compactness, forming a single solid mass, with no straggling or outlying portions; and it is strongly defended on almost every side by natural barriers offering great difficulties to an invader.

In comparison with the countries which formed the seats of the two monarchies already described, the general character of the Median territory is undoubtedly one of sterility. The high table-land is everywhere intersected by rocky ranges, spurs from Zagros, which have a general direction from west to east, and separate the country into a number of parallel broad valleys, or long plains, opening out into the desert. The appearance of these ranges is almost everywhere bare, arid, and forbidding. Above, they present to the eye huge masses of gray rock piled one upon another; below, a slope of detritus, destitute of trees or shrubs, and only occasionally nourishing a dry and scanty herbage. The appearance of the plains is little superior; they are flat and without undulations, composed in general of gravel or hard clay, and rarely enlivened by any show of water; except for two months in the spring, they exhibit to the eye a uniform brown expanse, almost treeless, which impresses the traveller with a feeling of sadness and weariness. Even in Azerbijan, which is one of the least arid portions of the territory, vast tracks consist of open undulating downs, desolate and sterile, bearing only a coarse withered grass and a few stunted bushes.

Still there are considerable exceptions to this general aspect of desolation. In the worst parts of the region there is a time after the spring rains when nature puts on a holiday dress, and the country becomes gay and cheerful. The slopes at the base of the rocky ranges are tinged with an emerald green: a richer vegetation springs up over the plains, which are covered with a fine herbage or with a variety of crops; the fruit trees which surround the villages burst out into the most luxuriant blossom; the roses come into bloom, and their perfume everywhere fills the air. For the two months of April and May the whole face of the country is changed, and a lovely verdure replaces the ordinary dull sterility.

In a certain number of more favored spots beauty and fertility are found during nearly the whole of the year. All round the shores of Lake Urumiyeh, more especially in the rich plain of Miyandab at its southern extremity, along the valleys of the Aras, the Kizil-uzen, and the Jaghetu, in the great valley of Linjan, fertilized by irrigation from the Zenderud, in the Zagros valleys, and in various other places, there is an excellent soil which produces abundantly with very slight cultivation.

The general sterility of Media arises from the scantiness of the water supply. It has but few rivers, and the streams that it possesses run for the most part in deep and narrow valleys sunk below the general level of the country, so that they cannot be applied at all widely to purposes of irrigation. Moreover, some of them are, unfortunately, impregnated with salt to such an extent that they are altogether useless for this purpose; and indeed, instead of fertilizing, spread around them desolation and barrenness. The only Median streams which are of sufficient importance to require description are the Aras, the Kizil-Uzen, the Jaghetu, the Aji-Su and the Zenderud, or river of Isfahan.

The Aras is only very partially a Median stream. It rises from several sources in the mountain tract between Kars and Erzeroum, and runs with a generally eastern direction through Armenia to the longitude of Mount Ararat, where it crosses the fortieth parallel and begins to trend southward, flowing along the eastern side of Ararat in a south-easterly direction, nearly to the Julfa ferry on the high road from Erivan to Tabriz. From this point it runs only a little south of east to long. 46° 30′ E. from Greenwich, when it makes almost a right angle and runs directly north-east to its junction with the Kur at Djavat. Soon after this it curves to the south, and enters the Caspian by several mouths in lat. 39° 10′ nearly. The Aras is a considerable stream almost from its source. At Hassan-Kaleh, less than twenty miles from Erzeroum, where the river is forded in several branches, the water reaches to the saddle-girths. At Keupri-Kieui, not much lower, the stream is crossed by a bridge of seven arches. At the Julfa ferry it is fifty yards wide, and runs with a strong current. At Megree, thirty miles further down, its width is eighty yards. In spring and early summer the stream receives enormous accessions from the spring rains and the melting of the snows, which produce floods that often cause great damage to the lands and villages along the valley. Hence the difficulty of maintaining bridges over the Aras, which was noted as early as the time of Augustus, and is attested by the ruins of many such structures remaining along its course. Still, there are at the present day at least three bridges over the stream—one, which has been already mentioned, at Keupri-Kieui, another a little above Nakshivan, and the third at Khudoperinski, a little below Megree. The length of the Aras, including only main windings, is 500 miles.

The Kizil-Uzen, or (as it is called in the lower part of its course) the Sefid-Rud, is a stream of less size than the Aras, but more important to Media, within which lies almost the whole of its basin. It drains a tract of 180 miles long by 150 broad before bursting through the Elburz mountain chain, and descending upon the low country which skirts the Caspian. Rising in Persian Kurdistan almost from the foot of Zagros, it runs in a meandering course with a general direction of north-east through that province into the district of Khamseh, where it suddenly sweeps round and flows in a bold curve at the foot of lofty and precipitous rocks, first northwest and then north, nearly to Miana, when it doubles back upon itself, and turning the flank of the Zenjan range runs with a course nearly south-east to Menjil, after which it resumes its original direction of north-east, and, rushing down the pass of Budbar, crosses Ghilan to the Caspian. Though its source is in direct distance no more than 320 miles from its mouth, its entire length, owing to its numerous curves and meanders, is estimated at 490 miles. It is a considerable stream, forded with difficulty, even in the dry season, as high up as Karagul, and crossed by a bridge of three wide arches before its junction with the Garongu river near Miana. In spring and early summer it is an impetuous torrent, and can only be forded within a short distance of its source.

The Jaghetu and the Aji-Su are the two chief rivers of the Urumiyeh basin. The Jaghetu rises from the foot of the Zagros chain, at a very little distance from the source of the Kizil-Uzen. It collects the streams from the range of hills which divides the Kizil-Uzen basin from that of Lake Urumiyeh, and flows in a tolerably straight course first north and then north-west to the south-eastern shore of the lake. Side by side with it for some distance flows the smaller stream of the Tatau, formed by torrents from Zagros; and between them, towards their mouths, is the rich plain of Miyandab, easily irrigated from the two streams, the level of whose beds is above that of the plain, and abundantly productive even under the present system of cultivation. The Aji-Su reaches the lake from the north-east. It rises from Mount Sevilan, within sixty miles of the Caspian, and flows with a course which is at first nearly due south, then north-west, and finally south-west, past the city of Tabriz, to the eastern shore of the lake, which it enters in lat. 37° 50′. The waters of the Aji-Su are, unfortunately, salt, and it is therefore valueless for purposes of irrigation.

The Zenderud or river of Isfahan rises from the eastern flank of the Kuh-i-Zerd (Yellow Mountain), a portion of the Bakhti-yari chain, and, receiving a number of tributaries from the same mountain district, flows with a course which is generally east or somewhat north of east, past the great city of Isfahan—so long the capital of Persia—into the desert country beyond, where it is absorbed in irrigation. Its entire course is perhaps not more than 120 or 130 miles; but running chiefly through a plain region, and being naturally a stream of large size, it is among the most valuable of the Median rivers, its waters being capable of spreading fertility, by means of a proper arrangement of canals, over a vast extent of country, and giving to this part of Iran a sylvan character, scarcely found elsewhere on the plateau.

It will be observed that of these streams there is not one which reaches the ocean. All the rivers of the great Iranic plateau terminate in lakes or inland seas, or else lose themselves in the desert. In general the thirsty sand absorbs, within a short distance of their source, the various brooks and streams which flow south and east into the desert from the northern and western mountain chains, without allowing them to collect into rivers or to carry fertility far into the plain region. The the river of Isfahan forms the only exception to this rule within the limits of the ancient Media. All its other important streams, as has been seen, flow either into the Caspian or into the great lake of Urumiyeh.

That lake itself now requires our attention. It is an oblong basin, stretching in its greater direction from N.N.W. to S.S. E., a distance of above eighty miles, with an average width of about twenty-five miles. On its eastern side a remarkable peninsula, projecting far into its waters, divides it into two portions of very unequal size—a northern and a southern.

The southern one, which is the largest of the two, is diversified towards its centre by a group of islands, some of which are of a considerable size. The lake, like others in this part of Asia, is several thousand feet above the sea level. Its waters are heavily impregnated with salt, resembling those of the Dead Sea. No fish can live in them. When a storm sweeps over their surface it only raises the waves a few feet; and no sooner is it passed than they rapidly subside again into a deep, heavy, death-like sleep. The lake is shallow, nowhere exceeding four fathoms, and averaging about two fathoms—a depth which, however, is rarely attained within two miles of the land. The water is pellucid. To the eye it has the deep blue color of some of the northern Italian lakes, whence it was called by the Armenians the Kapotan Zow or "Blue Sea."

According to the Armenian geography, Media contained eleven districts; Ptolemy makes the number eight; but the classical geographers in general are contented with the twofold division already indicated, and recognized at the constituent parts of Media only Atropatene (now Azerbijan) and Media Magna, a tract which nearly corresponds with the two provinces of Irak Ajemj and Ardelan. Of the minor subdivisions there are but two or three which seem to deserve any special notice. One of these is Ehagiana, or the tract skirting the Elburz Mountains from the vicinity of the Kizil-Uzen (or Sefid-Eud) to the Caspian Gates, a long and narrow slip, fairly productive, but excessively hot in summer, which took its name from the important city of Rhages. Another is Nissea, a name which the Medes seem to have carried with them from their early eastern abodes, and to have applied to some high upland plains west of the main chain of Zagros, which were peculiarly favorable to the breeding of horses. As Alexander visited these pastures on his way from Susa to Ecbatana, they must necessarily have lain to the south of the latter city. Most probably they are to be identified with the modern plains of Kbawah and Alishtar, between Behistun and Khorramabad, which are even now considered to afford the best summer pasturage in Persia.

It is uncertain whether any of these divisions were known in the time of the great Median Empire. They are not constituted in any case by marked natural lines or features. On the whole it is perhaps most probable that the main division—that into Media Magna and Media Atropatene—was ancient, Astropatene being the old home of the Medes, and Media Magna a later conquest; but the early political geography of the country is too obscure to justify us in laying down even this as certain. The minor political divisions are still less distinguishable in the darkness of those ancient times.

From the consideration of the districts which composed the Median territory, we may pass to that of their principal cities, some of which deservedly obtained a very great celebrity. Tho most important of all were the two Ecbatanas—the northern and the southern—which seem to have stood respectively in the position of metropolis to the northern and the southern province. Next to these may be named Rhages, which was probably from early times a very considerable place; while in the third rank may be mentioned Bagistan—rather perhaps a palace than a town—Concobar, Adrapan, Aspadan, Charax, Kudrus, Hyspaostes, Urakagabarna, etc.

The southern Ecbatana or Agbatana—which the Medes and Persians themselves knew as Hagmatan—was situated, as we learn from Polybius and Diodorus, on a plan at the foot of Mont Orontes, a little to the east of the Zagros range. The notices of these authors, combined with those of Eratosthenes, Isidore, Pliny, Arrian, and others, render it as nearly certain as possible that the site was that of the modern town of Hamadan, the name of which is clearly but a slight corruption of the true ancient appellation. [PLATE I., Fig. 2.] Mount Orontes is to be recognized in the modern Elwend or Erwend—a word etymologically identical with Oront-es—which is a long and lofty mountains standing out like a buttress from the Zagros range, with which it is connected towards the north-west, while on every other side it stands isolated, sweeping boldly down upon the flat country at its base. Copious streams descend from the mountain on every side, more particularly to the north-east, where the plain is covered with a carpet of the most luxuriant verdure, diversified with rills, and ornamented with numerous groves of large and handsome forest trees. It is here, on ground sloping slightly away from the roots of the mountain, that the modern town, which lies directly at its foot, is built. The ancient city, if we may believe Diodorus, did not approach the mountain within a mile or a mile and a half. At any rate, if it began where Hamadan now stands, it most certainly extended very much further into the plain. We need not suppose indeed that it had the circumference, or even half the circumference, which the Sicilian romancer assigns to it, since his two hundred and fifty stades would give a probable area of fifty square miles, more than double that of London! Ecbatana is not likely to have been at its most flourishing period a larger city than Nineveh; and we have already seen that Nineveh covered a space, within the walls, of not more than 1800 English acres.

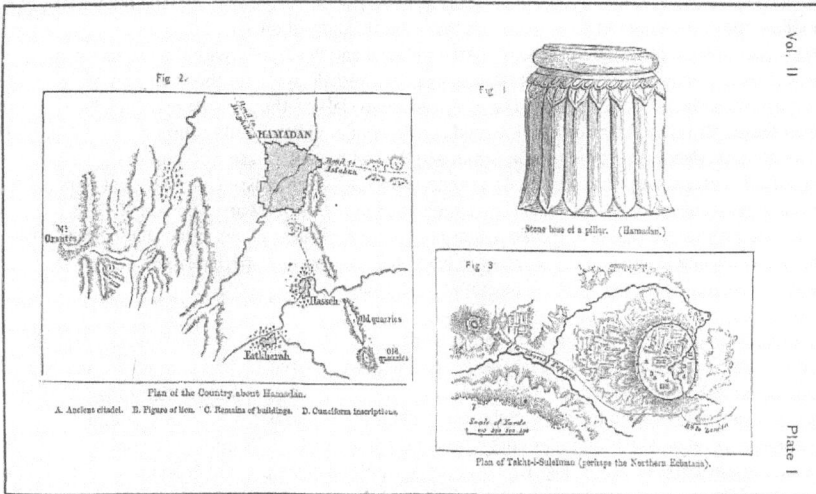

PLATE I

The character of the city and of its chief edifices has, unfortunately, to be gathered almost entirely from unsatisfactory authorities. Hitherto it has been found possible in these volumes to check and correct the statements of ancient writers, which are almost always exaggerated, by an appeal to the incontrovertible evidence of modern surveys and explorations. But the Median capital has never yet attracted a scientific expedition. The travellers by whom it has been visited have reported so unfavorably of its character as a field of antiquarian research that scarcely a spadeful of soil has been dug, either in the city or in its vicinity, with a view to recover traces of the ancient buildings. Scarcely any remains of antiquity are apparent. As the site has never been deserted, and the town has thus been subjected for nearly twenty-two centuries to the destructive ravages of foreign conquerors, and the still more injurious plunderings of native builders, anxious to obtain materials for new edifices at the least possible cost and trouble, the ancient structures have everywhere disappeared from sight, and are not even indicated by mounds of a sufficient size to attract the attention of common observers. Scientific explorers have consequently been deterred from turning their energies in this direction; more promising sites have offered and still offer themselves; and it is as yet uncertain whether the plan of the old town might not be traced and the position of its chief edifices fixed by the means of careful researches conducted by fully competent persons. In this dearth of modern materials we have to depend entirely upon the classical writers, who are rarely trustworthy in their descriptions or measurements, and who, in this instance, labor under the peculiar disadvantage of being mere reporters of the accounts given by others.

Ecbatana was chiefly celebrated for the magnificence of its palace, a structure ascribed by Diodorus to Semiramis, but most probably constructed originally by Cyaxares, and improved, enlarged, and embellished by the Achaemenian monarchs. According to the judicious and moderate Polybius, who prefaces his account by a protest against exaggeration and over-coloring, the circumference of the building was seven stades, or 1420 yards, somewhat more than four fifths of an English mile. This size, which a little exceeds that of the palace mound at Susa, while it is in its turn a little exceeded by the palatial platform at Persepolis, may well be accepted as probably close to the truth. Judging, however, from the analogy of the above-mentioned palaces, we must conclude that the area thus assigned to the royal residence was far from being entirely covered with buildings. One half of the space, perhaps more, would be occupied by large open courts, paved probably with marble, surrounding the various blocks of buildings and separating them from one another. The buildings themselves may be conjectured to have resembled those of the Achaemenian monarchs at Susa and Persepolis, with the exception, apparently, that the pillars, which formed their most striking characteristic, were for the most part of wood rather than of stone. Polybius distinguishes the pillars into two classes, those of the main buildings, and those which skirted the courts, from which it would appear that at Ecbatana the courts were surrounded by colonnades, as they were commonly in Greek and Roman houses. These wooden pillars, all either of cedar or of cypress, supported beams of a similar material, which crossed each other at right angles, leaving square spaces between, which were then filled in with woodwork. Above the whole a roof was placed, sloping at an angle, and composed (as we are told) of silver plates in the shape of tiles. The pillars, beams, and the rest of the woodwork were likewise coated with thin laminse of the precious metals, even gold being used for this purpose to a certain extent.

Such seems to have been the character of the true ancient Median palace, which served probably as a model to Darius and Xerxes when they designed their great palatial edifices at the more southern capitals. In the additions which the palace received under the Achaemenian kings, stone pillars may have been introduced; and hence probably the broken shafts and bases, so nearly resembling the Persepolitan, one of which Sir E. Ker Porter saw in the immediate neighborhood of Hamadan on his visit to that place in 1818. [PLATE I., Fig. 1.] But to judge from the description of Polybius, an older and ruder style of architecture prevailed in the main building, which depended for its effect not on the beauty of architectural forms, but on the richness and costliness of the material. A pillar architecture, so far as appears, began in this part of Asia with the Medes, who, however, were content to use the more readily obtained and more easily worked material of wood; while the Persians afterwards conceived the idea of substituting for these inartificial props the slender and elegant stone shafts which formed the glory of their grand edifices.

At a short distance from the palace was the "Acra," or citadel, an artificial structure, if we may believe Polybius, and a place of very remarkable strength. Here probably was the treasury, from which Darius Codomanus carried off 7000 talents of silver, when he fled towards Bactria for fear of Alexander. And here, too, may have been the Record Office, in which were deposited the royal decrees and other public documents under the earlier Persian kings. Some travellers are of opinion that a portion of the ancient structure still exists; and there is certainly a ruin on the outskirts of the modern town towards the south, which is known to the natives as "the inner fortress," and which may not improbably occupy some portion of the site whereon the original citadel stood. But the remains of building which now exist are certainly not of an earlier date than the era of Parthian supremacy, and they can therefore throw no light on the character of the old Median stronghold. It may be thought perhaps that the description which Herodotus gives of the building called by him "the palace of Deioces" should be here applied, and that by its means we might obtain an exact notion of the original structure. But the account of this author is wholly at variance with the natural features of the neighborhood, where there is no such conical hill as he describes, but only a plain surrounded by mountains. It seems, therefore, to be certain that either his description is a pure myth, or that it applies to another city, the Ecbatana of the northern province. It is doubtful whether the Median capital was at any time surrounded with walls. Polybius expressly declares that it was an unwalled place in his day and there is some reason to suspect that it had always been in this condition. The Medes and Persians appear to have been in general content to establish in each town a fortified citadel or stronghold, round which the houses were clustered, without superadding the further defence of a town wall. Ecbatana accordingly seems never to have stood a siege. When the nation which held it was defeated in the open field, the city (unlike Babylon and Nineveh) submitted to the conqueror without a struggle. Thus the marvellous description in the book of Judith, which is internally very improbable, would appear to be entirely destitute of any, even the slightest, foundation in fact.

The chief city of northern Media, which bore in later times the names of Gaza, Gazaca, or Canzaca, is thought to have also been called Ecbatana, and to have been occasionally mistaken by the Greeks for the southern or real capital. The description of Herodotus, which is irreconcilably at variance with the local features of the Hamadan site, accords sufficiently with the existing remains of a considerable city in the province of Azerbijan; and it seems certainly to have been a city in these parts which was called by Moses of Chorene "the second Ecbatana, the seven-walled town." The peculiarity of this place was its situation on and about a conical hill which sloped gently down from its summit to its base, and allowed of the interposition of seven circuits of wall between the plain and the hill's crest. At the top of the hill, within the innermost circle of the defences, were the Royal Palace and the treasuries; the sides of the hill were occupied solely by the fortifications; and at the base, outside the circuit of the outermost wall, were the domestic and other buildings which constituted the town. According to the information received by Herodotus, the battlements which crowned the walls were variously colored. Those of the outer circle were white, of the next black, of the third scarlet, of the fourth blue, of the fifth orange, of the sixth silver, and of the seventh gold. A pleasing or at any rate a striking effect was thus produced— the citadel, which towered above the town, presenting to the eye seven distinct rows of colors.

If there was really a northern as well as a southern Ecbatana, and if the account of Herodotus, which cannot possibly apply to the southern capital, may be regarded as truly describing the great city of the north, we may with much probability fix the site of the northern town at the modern Takht-i-Suleiman, in the upper valley of the Saruk, a tributary of the Jaghetu. [PLATE I., Fig. 3.] Here alone in northern Media are there important ruins occupying such a position as that which Herodotus describes. Near the head of a valley in which runs the main branch of the Saruk, at the edge of the hills which skirt it to the north, there stands a conical mound projecting into the vale and rising above its surface to the height of 150 feet. The geological formation of the mound is curious in the extreme. It seems to owe its origin entirely to a small lake, the waters of which are so strongly impregnated with calcareous matter that wherever they overflow they rapidly form a deposit which is as hard and firm as natural rock. If the lake was originally on a level with the valley, it would soon have formed incrustations round its edge, which every casual or permanent overflow would have tended to raise; and thus, in the course of ages, the entire hill may have been formed by a mere accumulation of petrefactions. The formation would progress more or less rapidly according to the tendency of the lake to overflow its bounds; which tendency must have been strong until the water reached its present natural level—the level, probably, of some other sheet of water in the hills, with which it is connected by an underground siphon. The lake, which is of an irregular shape, is about 300 paces in circumference. Its water, notwithstanding the quantity of mineral matter held in solution, is exquisitely clear, and not unpleasing to the taste. Formerly it was believed by the natives to be unfathomable; but experiments made in 1837 showed the depth to be no more than 156 feet.

The ruins which at present occupy this remarkable site consist of a strong wall, guarded by numerous bastions and pierced by four gateways, which runs round the brow of the hill in a slightly irregular ellipse, of some interesting remains of buildings within this walled space, and of a few insignificant traces of inferior edifices on the slope between the plain and the summit. As it is not thought that any of these remains are of a date anterior to the Sassanian kingdom, no description will be given of them here. We are only concerned with the Median city, and that has entirely disappeared. Of the seven walls, one alone is to be traced; and even here the Median structure has perished, and been replaced by masonry of a far later age. Excavations may hereafter bring, to light some remnants of the original town, but at present research has done no more than recover for us a forgotten site.

The Median city next in importance to the two Ecbatanas was Raga or Rhages, near the Caspian Gates, almost at the extreme eastern limits of the territory possessed by the Medes.

The great antiquity of this place is marked by its occurrence in the Zendavesta among the primitive settlements of the Arians. Its celebrity during the time of the Empire is indicated by the position which it occupies in the romances of Tobit and Judith. It maintained its rank under the Persians, and is mentioned by Darius Hystaspis as the scene of the struggle which terminated the great Median revolt. The last Darius seems to have sent thither his heavy baggage and the ladies of his court, when he resolved to quit Ecbatana and fly eastward. It has been already noticed that Rhages gave name to a district; and this district maybe certainly identified with the long narrow tract of fertile territory intervening between the Elburz mountain-range and the desert, from about Kasvin to Khaar, or from long. 30° to 52° 30'. The exact site of the city of Rhages within this territory is somewhat doubtful. All accounts place it near the eastern extremity; and as there are in this direction ruins of a town called Rhei or Rhey, it has been usual to assume that they positively fix the locality. But similarity, or even identity, of name is an insufficient proof of a site; and, in the present instance, there are grounds for placing Rhages very much nearer to the Caspian Gates than the position of Rhei. Arrian, whose accuracy is notorious, distinctly states that from the Gates to Rhages was only a single day's march, and that Alexander accomplished the distance in that time. Now from Rhei to the Girduni Surdurrah pass, which undoubtedly represents the Pylae Cacpise of Arrian, is at least fifty miles, a distance which no army could accomplish in less time than two days. Rhages consequently must have been considerably to the east of Rhei, about half-way between it and the celebrated pass which it was considered to guard. Its probable position is the modern Kaleh Erij, near Veramin, about 23 miles from the commencement of the Surdurrah pass, where there are considerable remains of an ancient town.

In the same neighborhood with Rhages, but closer to the Straits, perhaps on the site now occupied by the ruins known as Uewanukif, or possibly even nearer to the foot of the pass, was the Median city of

Charax, a place not to be confounded with the more celebrated city called Gharax Spasini, the birthplace of Dionysius the geographer, which was on the Persian Gulf, at the mouth of the Tigris.

The other Median cities, whose position can be determined with an approach to certainty, were in the western portion of the country, in the range of Zagros, or in the fertile tract between that range and the desert. The most important of these are Bagistan, Adrapan, Concobar, and Aspadan.

Bagistan is described by Isidore as a "city situated on a hill, where there was a pillar and a statue of Semiramis." Diodorus has an account of the arrival of Semiramis at the place, of her establishing a royal park or paradise in the plain below the mountain, which was watered by an abundant spring, of her smoothing the face of the rock where it descended precipitously upon the low ground, and of her carving on the surface thus obtained her own effigy, with an inscription in Assyrian characters. The position assigned to Bagistan by both writers, and the description of Diodorus, identify the place beyond a doubt with the now famous Behistun, where the plain, the fountain, the precipitous rock, and the scarped surface are still to be seen, through the supposed figure of Semiramis, her pillar, and her inscription have disappeared. [PLATE II., Fig. 1.] This remarkable spot, lying on the direct route between Babylon and Ecbatana, and presenting the unusual combination of a copious fountain, a rich plain, and a rock suitable for sculptures, must have early attracted the attention of the great monarchs who marched their armies through the Zagros range, as a place where they might conveniently set up memorials of their exploits. The works of this kind ascribed by the ancient writers to Semiramis were probably either Assyrian or Babylonian, and (it is most likely) resembled the ordinary monuments which the kings of Babylon and Nineveh delighted to erect in countries newly conquered. The example set by the Mesopotamians was followed by their Arian neighbors, when the supremacy passed into their hands; and the famous mountain, invested by them with a sacred character, was made to subserve and perpetuate their glory by receiving sculptures and inscriptions which showed them to have become the lords of Asia. The practice did not even stop here. When the Parthian kingdom of the Arsacidee had established itself in these parts at the expense of the Seleucidse, the rock was once more called upon to commemorate the warlike triumphs of a new race. Gotarzes, the contemporary of the Emperor Claudius, after defeating his rival Meherdates in the plain between Behistun and Kermanshah, inscribed upon the mountain, which already bore the impress of the great monarchs of Assyria and Persia, a record of his recent victory.

The name of Adrapan occurs only in Isidore, who places it between Bagistan and Ecbatana, at the distance of twelve schoeni—36 Roman or 34 British miles from the latter. It was, he says, the site of an ancient palace belonging to Ecbatana, which Tigranes the Armenian had destroyed. The name and situation sufficiently identify Adrapan with the modern village of Arteman, which lies on the southern face of Elwend near its base, and is well adapted for a royal residence. Here, during the severest winter, when Hamadan and the surrounding country are buried in snow, a warm and sunny climate is to be found; whilst in the summer a thousand rills descending from Elwend diffuse around fertility and fragrance. Groves of trees grow up in rich luxuriance from the well-irrigated soil, whose thick foliage affords a welcome shelter from the heat of the noonday sun. The climate, the gardens, and the manifold blessings of the place are proverbial throughout Persia; and naturally caused the choice of the site for a retired palace, to which the court of Ecbatana might adjourn when either the summer heat and dust or the winter cold made residence in the capital irksome.

In the neighborhood of Adrapan, on the road leading to Bagistan, stood Concobar, which is undoubtedly the modern Kungawar, and perhaps the Chavon of Diodorus. Here, according to the Sicilian historian, Semiramis built a palace and laid out a paradise; and here, in the time of Isidore, was a famous temple of Artemis. Colossal ruins crown the summit of the acclivity on which the town of Kungawar stands, which may be the remains of this latter building; but no trace has been found that can be regarded as either Median or Assyrian.

Plate II.

Vol. II.

Fig. 1.

View of the Rock of Behistun.

Fig. 2

View in Mazanderan—the Caspian Sea in the distance.

PLATE II

The Median town of Aspadan, which is mentioned by no writer but Ptolemy, would scarcely deserve notice here, if it were not for its modern celebrity. Aspadan, corrupted into Isfahan, became the capital of Persia, under the Sen kings, who rendered it one of the most magnificent cities of Asia. It is uncertain whether it existed at all in the time of the great Median empire. If so, it was, at best, an outlying town of little consequence on the extreme southern confines of the territory, where it abutted upon Persia proper. The district wherein it lay was inhabited by the Median tribe of the Parastaceni.

Upon the whole it must be allowed that the towns of Media were few and of no great account. The Medes did not love to congregate in large cities, but preferred to scatter themselves in villages over their broad and varied territory. The protection of walls, necessary for the inhabitants of the low Mesopotamian regions, was not required by a people whose country was full of natural fastnesses to which they could readily remove on the approach of danger. Excepting the capital and the two important cities of Gazaca and Rhages, the Median towns were insignificant. Even those cities themselves were probably of moderate dimensions, and had little of the architectural splendor which gives so peculiar an interest to the towns of Mesopotamia. Their principal buildings were in a frail and perishable material, unsuited to bear the ravages of time; they have consequently altogether disappeared, and in the whole of Media modern researches have failed to bring to light a single edifice which can be assigned with any show of probability to the period of the Empire.

The plan adopted in former portions of this work makes it necessary, before concluding this chapter, to glance briefly at the character of the various countries and districts by which Media was bordered—the Caspian district upon the north, Armenia upon the north-west, the Zagros region and Assyria upon the west, Persia proper upon the south, and upon the east Sagartia and Parthia.

North and north-east of the mountain range which under different names skirts the southern shores of the Caspian Sea and curves round its south-western corner, lies a narrow but important strip of territory—the modern Ghilan and Mazanderan. [PLATE II., Fig. 2.] This is a most fertile region, well watered and richly wooded, and forms one of the most valuable portions of the modern kingdom of Persia. At first it is a low flat tract of deep alluvial soil, but little raised above the level of the Caspian; gradually however it rises into swelling hills which form the supports of the high mountains that shut in this sheltered region, a region only to be reached by a very few passes over or through them. The mountains are clothed on this side nearly to their summit with dwarf oaks, or with shrubs and brushwood; while, lower down, their flanks are covered with forests of elms, cedars, chestnuts, beeches, and cypress trees. The gardens and orchards of the natives are of the most superb character; the vegetation is luxuriant; lemons, oranges, peaches, pomegranates, besides other fruits, abound; rice, hemp, sugar-canes, mulberries are cultivated with success; vines grow wild; and the valleys are strewn with flowers of rare fragrance, among which may be noted the rose, the honeysuckle, and the sweetbrier. Nature, however, with her usual justice, has balanced these extraordinary advantages with peculiar drawbacks; the tiger, unknown in any other part of Western Asia, here lurks in the thickets, ready to spring at any moment on the unwary traveller; inundations are frequent, and carry desolation far and wide; the waters, which thus escape from the river beds, stagnate in marshes, and during the summer and autumn heats pestilential exhalations arise, which destroy the stranger, and bring even the acclimatized native to the brink of the grave. The Persian monarch chooses the southern rather than the northern side of the mountains for the site of his capital, preferring the keen winter cold and dry summer heat of the high and almost waterless plateau to the damp and stifling air of the low Caspian region.

The narrow tract of which this is a description can at no time have sheltered a very numerous or powerful people. During the Median period, and for many ages afterwards, it seems to have been inhabited by various petty tribes of predatory habits—Cadusians, Mardi, Tapyri, etc.,—who passed their time in petty quarrels among themselves, and in plundering raids upon their great southern neighbor. Of these tribes the Cadusians alone enjoyed any considerable reputation. They were celebrated for their skill with the javelin—a skill probably represented by the modern Persian use of the djereed. According to Diodorus, they were engaged in frequent wars with the Median kings, and were able to bring into the field a force of 200,000 men! Under the Persians they seem to have been considered good soldiers, and to have sometimes made a struggle for independence. But there is no real reason to believe that they were of such strength as to have formed at any time a danger to the Median kingdom, to which it is more probable that they generally acknowledged a qualified subjection.

The great country of Armenia, which lay north-west and partly north of Media, has been generally described in the first volume; but a few words will be here added with respect to the more eastern portion, which immediately bordered upon the Median territory. This consisted of two outlying districts, separated from the rest of the country, the triangular basin of Lake Van, and the tract between the Kur and Aras rivers—the modern Karabagh and Erivan. The basin of Lake Van, surrounded by high ranges, and forming the very heart of the mountain system of this part of Asia, is an isolated region, a sort of natural citadel, where a strong military power would be likely to establish itself. Accordingly it is here, and here alone in all Armenia, that we find signs of the existence, during the Assyrian and Median periods, of a great organized monarchy.

The Van inscriptions indicate to us a line of kings who bore sway in the eastern Armenia—the true Ararat—and who were both in civilization and in military strength far in advance of any of the other princes who divided among them the Armenian territory. The Van monarchs may have been at times formidable enemies of the Medes. They have left traces of their dominion, not only on the tops of the mountain passes which lead into the basin of Lake Urumiyeh, but even in the comparatively low plain of Miyandab on the southern shore of that inland sea. It is probable from this that they were at one time masters of a large portion of Media Atropatene, and the very name of Urumiyeh, which still attaches to the lake, may have been given to it from one of their tribes. In the tract between the Kur and Aras, on the other hand, there is no sign of the early existence of any formidable power. Here the mountains are comparatively low, the soil is fertile, and the climate temperate. The character of the region would lead its inhabitants to cultivate the arts of peace rather than those of war, and would thus tend to prevent them from being formidable or troublesome to their neighbors.

The Zagros region, which in the more ancient times separated between Media and Assyria, being inhabited by a number of independent tribes, but which was ultimately absorbed into the more powerful country, requires no notice here, having been sufficiently described among the tracts by which Assyria was bordered. At first a serviceable shield to the weak Arian tribes which were establishing themselves along its eastern base upon the high plateau, it gradually passed into their possession as they increased in strength, and ultimately became a main nursery of their power, furnishing to their armies vast numbers both of men and horses. The great horse pastures, from which the Medes first and the Persians afterwards, supplied their numerous and excellent cavalry, were in this quarter; and the troops which it furnished—hardy mountaineers accustomed to brave the severity of a most rigorous climate—must have been among the most effective of the Median forces.

On the south Media was bounded by Persia proper—a tract which corresponded nearly with the modern province of Farsistan. The complete description of this territory, the original seat of the Persian nation, belongs to a future volume of this work, which will contain an account of the "Fifth Monarchy." For the present it is sufficient to observe that the Persian territory was for the most part a highland, very similar to Media, from which it was divided by no strongly marked line or natural boundary. The Persian mountains are a continuation of the Zagros chain, and Northern Persia is a portion—the southern portion—of the same great plateau, whose western and north-western skirts formed the great mass of the Median territory. Thus upon this side Media was placed in the closest connection with an important country, a country similar in character to her own, where a hardy race was likely to grow up, with which she might expect to have difficult contests.

Finally, towards the east lay the great salt desert, sparsely inhabited by various nomadic races, among which the most important were the Cossseans and the Sagartians. To the latter people Herodotus seems to assign almost the whole of the sandy region, since he unites them with the Sarangians and Thamanseans on the one hand, with the Utians and Mycians upon the other. They were a wild race, probably of Arian origin, who hunted with the lasso over the great desert mounted on horses, and could bring into the field a force of eight or ten thousand men. Their country, a waste of sand and gravel, in parts thickly encrusted with salt, was impassable to an army, and formed a barrier which effectively protected Media along the greater portion of her eastern frontier. Towards the extreme north-east the Sagartians were replaced by the Cossseans and the Parthians, the former probably the people of the Siah-Koh mountain, the latter the inhabitants of the tract known now as the Atak, or "skirt," which extends along the southern flank of the Elburz range from the Caspian Gates nearly to Herat, and is capable of sustaining a very considerable population. The Cossseans were plunderers, from whose raids Media suffered constant annoyance; but they were at no time of sufficient strength to cause any serious fear. The Parthians, as we learn from the course of events, had in them the materials of a mighty people; but the hour for their elevation and expansion was not yet come, and the keenest observer of Median times could scarcely have perceived in them the future lords of Western Asia. From Parthia, moreover, Media was divided by the strong rocky spur which runs out from the Elburz into the desert in long. 52° 10' nearly, over which is the narrow pass already mentioned as the Caspian Gates. Thus Media on most sides was guarded by the strong natural barriers of seas, mountains, and deserts lying open only on the south, where she adjoined upon a kindred people. Her neighbors were for the most part weak in numbers, though warlike. Armenia, however, to the north-west, Assyria to the west, and Persia to the south, were all more or less formidable. A prescient eye might have foreseen that the great struggles of Media would be with these powers, and that if she attained imperial proportions it must be by their subjugation or absorption.

CHAPTER II

CLIMATE AND PRODUCTIONS

Media, like Assyria, is a country of such extent and variety that, in order to give a correct description of its climate, we must divide it into regions. Azerbijan, or Atropatene, the most northern portion, has a climate altogether cooler than the rest of Media; while in the more southern division of the country there is a marked difference between the climate of the east and of the west, of the tracts lying on the high plateau and skirting the Great Salt Desert, and of those contained within or closely abutting upon the Zagros mountain range. The difference here is due to the difference of physical conformation, which is as great as possible, the broad mountainous plains about Kasvin, Koum, and Kashan, divided from each other by low rocky ridges, offering the strongest conceivable contrast to the perpetual alternations of mountain and valley, precipitous height and deep wooded glen, which compose the greater part of the Zagros region.

The climate of Azerbijan is temperate and pleasant, though perhaps somewhat overwarm, in summer; while in winter it is bitterly severe, colder than that of almost any other region in the same latitude. This extreme rigor seems to be mainly owing to elevation, the very valleys and valley plains of the tract being at a height of from 4000 to 5000 feet above the sea level. Frost commonly sets in towards the end of November—or at latest early in December; snow soon covers the ground to the depth of several feet; the thermometer falls below zero; the sun shines brightly except when from time to time fresh deposits of snow occur; but a keen and strong wind usually prevails, which is represented as "cutting like a sword," and being a very "assassin of life." Deaths from cold are of daily occurrence; and it is impossible to travel without the greatest risk. Whole companies or caravans occasionally perish beneath the drift, when the wind is violent, especially if a heavy fall happen to coincide with one of the frequent easterly gales. The severe weather commonly continues till March, when travelling becomes possible, but the snow remains on much of the ground till May, and on the mountains still longer. The spring, which begins in April, is temperate and delightful; a sudden burst of vegetation succeeds to the long winter lethargy; the air is fresh and balmy, the sun pleasantly warm, the sky generally cloudless. In the month of May the heat increases—thunder hangs in the air—and the valleys are often close and sultry. Frequent showers occur, and the hail-storms are sometimes so violent as to kill the cattle in the fields. As the summer advances the heats increase, but the thermometer rarely reaches 90° in the shade, and except in the narrow valleys the air is never oppressive. The autumn is generally very fine. Foggy mornings are common; but they are succeeded by bright pleasant days, without wind or rain. On the whole the climate is pronounced healthy, though somewhat trying to Europeans, who do not readily adapt themselves to a country where the range of the thermometer is as much as 90° or 100°. In the part of Media situated on the great plateau—the modern Irak Ajemi—in which are the important towns of Teheran, Isfahan, Hamadan, Kashan, Kasvin, and Koum. the climate is altogether warmer than in Azerbijan, the summers being hotter, and the winters shorter and much less cold. Snow indeed covers the ground for about three months, from early in December till March; but the thermometer rarely shows more than ten or twelve degrees of frost, and death from cold is uncommon. The spring sets in about the beginning of March, and is at first somewhat cool, owing to the prevalence of the baude caucasan or north wind,a which blows from districts where the snow still lies. But after a little time the weather becomes delicious; the orchards are a mass of blossom; the rose gardens come into bloom; the cultivated lands are covered with springing crops; the desert itself wears a light livery of green. Every sense is gratified; the nightingale bursts out with a full gush of song; the air plays softly upon the cheek, and comes loaded with fragrance. Too soon, however, this charming time passes away, and the summer heats begin, in some places as early as June 18 The thermometer at midday rises to 90 or 100 degrees. Hot gusts blow from the desert, sometimes with great violence. The atmosphere is described as choking; and in parts of the plateau it is usual for the inhabitants to quit their towns almost in a body, and retire for several months into the mountains. This extreme heat is, however, exceptional; in most parts of the plateau the summer warmth is tempered by cool breezes from the surrounding mountains, on which there is always a good deal of snow. At Hamadan, which, though on the plain, is close to the mountains, the thermometer seems scarcely ever to rise above 90°, and that degree of heat is attained only for a few hours in the day. The mornings and evenings are cool and refreshing; and altogether the climate quite justifies the choice of the Persian monarchs, who selected Ecbatana for their place of residence during the hottest portion of the year. Even at Isfahan, which is on the edge of the desert, the heat is neither extreme nor prolonged. The hot gusts which blow from the east and from the south raise the temperature at times nearly to a hundred degrees; but these oppressive winds alternate with cooler breezes from the west, often accompanied by rain; and the average highest temperature during the day in the hottest month, which is August, does not exceed 90°.

A peculiarity in the climate of the plateau which deserves to be noticed is the extreme dryness of the atmosphere. In summer the rains which fall are slight, and they are soon absorbed by the thirsty soil. There is a little dew at nights, especially in the vicinity of the few streams; but it disappears with the first hour of sunshine, and the air is left without a particle of moisture. In winter the dryness is equally great; frost taking the place of heat, with the same effect upon the atmosphere. Unhealthy exhalations are thus avoided, and the salubrity of the climate is increased; but the European will sometimes sigh for the soft, balmy airs of his own land, which have come flying over the sea, and seem to bring their wings still dank with the ocean spray.

Another peculiarity of this region, produced by the unequal rarefaction of the air over its different portions, is the occurrence, especially in spring and summer, of sudden gusts, hot or cold, which blow with great violence. These gusts are sometimes accompanied with, whirlwinds, which sweep the country in different directions, carrying away with them leaves, branches, stubble, sand, and other light substances, and causing great annoyance to the traveller. They occur chiefly in connection with a change of wind, and are no doubt consequent on the meeting of two opposite currents. Their violence, however, is moderate, compared with that of tropical tornadoes, and it is not often that they do any considerable damage to the crops over which they sweep.

One further characteristic of the flat region may be noticed. The intense heat of the summer sun striking on the dry sand or the saline efflorescence of the desert throws the air over them into such a state of quivering undulation as produces the most wonderful and varying effects, distorting the forms of objects, and rendering the most familiar strange and hard to be recognized. A mud bank furrowed by the rain will exhibit the appearance of a magnificent city, with columns, domes, minarets, and pyramids; a few stunted bushes will be transformed into a forest of stately trees; a distant mountain will, in the space of a minute, assume first the appearance of a lofty peak, then swell out at the top, and resemble a mighty mushroom, next split into several parts, and finally settle down into a flat tableland. Occasionally, though not very often that semblance of water is produced which Europeans are are apt to suppose the usual effect of mirage. The images of objects are reflected at their base in an inverted position; the desert seems converted into a vast lake; and the thirsty traveller, advancing towards it, finds himself the victim of an illusion, which is none the less successful because he has been a thousand times forewarned of its deceptive power.

In the mountain range or Zagros and the tracts adjacent to it, the climate, owing to the great differences of elevation, is more varied than in the other parts of the ancient Media. Severe cold prevails in the higher mountain regions for seven months out of the twelve, while during the remaining five the heat is never more than moderate. In the low valleys, on the contrary, and in other favored situations, the winters are often milder than on the plateau; while in the summers, if the heat is not greater, at any rate it is more oppressive. Owing to the abundance of the streams and proximity of the melting snows, the air is moist; and the damp heat, which stagnates in the valleys, broods fever and ague. Between these extremes of climate and elevation, every variety is to be found; and, except in winter, a few hours' journey will almost always bring the traveller into a temperate region.

In respect of natural productiveness, Media (as already observed) differs exceedingly in different, and even in adjacent, districts. The rocky ridges of the great plateau, destitute of all vegetable mold, are wholly bare and arid, admitting not the slightest degree of cultivation. Many of the mountains of Azerbijan, naked, rigid, and furrowed, may compare even with these desert ranges for sterility. The higher parts of Zagros and Elburz are sometimes of the same character; but more often they are thickly clothed with forests, affording excellent timber and other valuable commodities. In the Elburz pines are found near the summit, while lower down there occur, first the wild almond and the dwarf oak, and then the usual timber-trees of the country, the Oriental plane, the willow, the poplar, and the walnut. The walnut grows to a large size both here and in Azerbijan, but the poplar is the wood most commonly used for building purposes. In Zagros, besides most of these trees, the ash and the terebinth or turpentine-tree are common; the oak bears gall-nuts of a large size; and the gum-tragacanth plant frequently clothes the mountain-sides. The valleys of this region are full of magnificent orchards, as are the low grounds and more sheltered nooks of Azerbijan. The fruit-trees comprise, besides vines and mulberries, the apple, the pear, the quince, the plum, the cherry, the almond, the nut, the chestnut, the olive, the peach, the nectarine, and the apricot.

On the plains of the high plateau there is a great scarcity of vegetation. Trees of a large size grow only in the few places which are well watered, as in the neighborhood of Hamadan, Isfahan, and in a less degree of Kashan. The principal tree is the Oriental plane, which flourishes together with poplars and willows along the water-courses; cypresses also grow freely; elms and cedars are found, and the orchards and gardens contain not only the fruit-trees mentioned above, but also the jujube, the cornel, the filbert, the medlar, the pistachio nut, the pomegranate, and the fig. Away from the immediate vicinity of the rivers and the towns, not a tree, scarcely a bush, is to be seen. The common thorn is indeed tolerably abundant in a few places; but elsewhere the tamarisk and a few other sapless shrubs are the only natural products of this bare and arid region.

In remarkable contrast with the natural barrenness of this wide tract are certain favored districts in Zagros and Azerbijan, where the herbage is constant throughout the summer, and sometimes only too luxuriant. Such are the rich and extensive grazing grounds of Khawah and Alishtar, near Kermanshah, the pastures near Ojan and Marand, and the celebrated Chowal Moghan or plain of Moghan, on the lower course of the Araxes river, where the grass is said to grow sufficiently high to cover a man on horseback. These, however, are rare exceptions to the general character of the country, which is by nature unproductive, and scarcely deserving even of the qualified encomium of Strabo.

Still Media, though deficient in natural products, is not ill adapted for cultivation. The Zagros valleys and hillsides produce under a very rude system of agriculture, besides the fruits already noticed, rice, wheat, barley, millet, sesame, Indian corn, cotton, tobacco, mulberries, cucumbers, melons, pumpkins, and the castor-oilplant. In Azerbijan the soil is almost all cultivable, and if ploughed and sown will bring good crops of the ordinary kinds of grain. Even on the side of the desert, where Nature has shown herself most niggardly, and may seem perhaps to deserve the reproach of Cicero, that she behaves as a step mother to a man rather than as a mother, a certain amount of care and scientific labor may render considerable tracts fairly productive. The only want of this region is water; and if the natural deficiency of this necessary fluid can be anyhow supplied, all parts of the plateau will bear crops, except those which form the actual Salt Desert. In modern, and still more in ancient times, this fact has been clearly perceived, and an elaborate system of artifical irrigation, suitable to the peculiar circumstances of the country, has been very widely established. The system of kanats, as they are called at the present day, aims at utilizing to the uttermost all the small streams and rills which descend towards the desert from the surrounding mountains, and at conveying as far as possible into the plain the spring water, which is the indispensable condition of cultivation in a country where—except for a few days in the spring and autumn—rain scarcely ever falls. As the precious element would rapidly evaporate if exposed to the rays of the summer sun, the Iranian husbandman carries his conduit underground, laboriously tunnelling through the stiff argillaceous soil, at a depth of many feet below the surface. The mode in which he proceeds is as follows. At intervals along the line of his intended conduit he first sinks shafts, which he then connects with one another by galleries, seven or eight feet in height, giving his galleries a slight incline, so that the water may run down them freely, and continuing them till he reaches a point where he wishes to bring the water out upon the surface of the plain. Here and there, at the foot of his shafts, he digs wells, from which the fluid can readily be raised by means of a bucket and a windlass; and he thus brings under cultivation a considerable belt of land along the whole line of the kanat, as well as a large tract at its termination. These conduits, on which the cultivation of the plateau depends, were established at so remote a date that they were popularly ascribed to the mythic Semiramis, the supposed wife of Ninus. It is thought that in ancient times they were longer and more numerous than at present, when they occur only occasionally, and seldom extend more than a few miles from the base of the hills.

By help of the irrigation thus contrived, the great plateau of Iran will produce good crops of grain, rice, wheat, barley, Indian corn, doura, millet, and sesame. It will also bear cotton, tobacco, saffron, rhubarb, madder, poppies which give a good opium, senna, and assafoetida. Its garden vegetables are excellent, and include potatoes, cabbages, lentils, kidney-beans, peas, turnips, carrots, spinach, beetroot, and cucumbers. The variety of its fruit-trees has been already noticed. The flavor of their produce is in general good, and in some cases surpassingly excellent. No quinces are so fine as those of Isfahan, and no melons have a more delicate flavor. The grapes of Kasvin are celebrated, and make a remarkably good wine.

Among the flowers of the country must be noted, first of all, its roses, which flourish in the most luxuriant abundance, and are of every variety of hue. The size to which the tree will grow is extraordinary, standards sometimes exceeding the height of fourteen or fifteen feet. Lilacs, jasmines, and many other flowering shrubs are common in the gardens, while among wild flowers may be noticed hollyhocks, lilies, tulips, crocuses, anemones, lilies of the valley, fritillaries, gentians, primroses, convolvuluses, chrysanthemums, heliotropes, pinks, water-lilies, ranunculuses, jonquils, narcissuses, hyacinths, mallows, stocks, violets, a fine campanula (Michauxia levigata), a mint (Nepeta longiflora), several sages, salsolas, and fagonias. In many places the wild flowers during the spring months cover the ground, painting it with a thousand dazzling or delicate hues.

The mineral products of Media are numerous and valuable. Excellent stone of many kinds abounds in almost every part of the country, the most important and valuable being the famous Tabriz marble. This curious substance appears to be a petrifaction formed by natural springs, which deposit carbonate of lime in large quantities. It is found only in one place, on the flanks of the hills, not far from the Urumiyeh lake. The slabs are used for tombstones, for the skirting of rooms, and for the pavements of baths and palaces; when cut thin they often take the place of glass in windows, being semi-transparent. The marble is commonly of a pale yellow color, but occasionally it is streaked with red, green, or copper-colored veins.

In metals the country is thought to be rich, but no satisfactory examination of it has been as yet made. Iron, copper, and native steel are derived from mines actually at work; while Europeans have observed indications of lead, arsenic, and antimony in Azerbijan, in Kurdistan, and in the rocky ridges which intersect the desert. Tradition speaks of a time when gold and silver were procured from mountains near Takht-i-Suleman, and it is not unlikely that they may exist both there and in the Zagros range. Quartz, the well-known matrix of the precious metal, abounds in Kurdistan.

Of all the mineral products, none is more abundant than salt. On the side of the desert, and again near Tabriz at the mouth of the Aji Su, are vast plains which glisten with the substance, and yield it readily to all who care to gather it up. Saline springs and streams are also numerous, from which salt can be obtained by evaporation. But, besides these sources of supply, rock salt is found in places, and this is largely quarried, and is preferred by the natives.

Other important products of the earth are saltpetre, which is found in the Elburz, and in Azerbijan; sulphur, which abounds in the same regions, and likewise on the high plateau; alum, which is quarried near Tabriz; naphtha and gypsum, which are found in Kurdistan; and talc, which exists in the mountains near Koum, in the vicinity of Tabriz, and probably in other places.

The chief wild animals which have been observed within the limits of the ancient Media are the lion, the tiger, the leopard, the bear, the beaver, the jackal, the wolf, the wild ass, the ibex or wild goat, the wild sheep, the stag, the antelope, the wild boar, the fox, the hare, the rabbit, the ferret, the rat, the jerboa, the porcupine, the mole, and the marmot. The lion and tiger are exceedingly rare; they seem to be found only in Azerbijan, and we may perhaps best account for their presence there by considering that a few of these animals occasionally stray out of Mazanderan, which is their only proper locality in this part of Asia. Of all the beasts, the most abundant are the stag and the wild goat, which are numerous in the Elburz, and in parts of Azerbijan, the wild boar, which abounds both in Azerbijan, and in the country about Hamadan, and the jackal, which is found everywhere. Bears flourish in Zagros, antelopes in

Azerbijan, in the Elburz, and on the plains near Sultaniyeh. The wild ass is found only in the desert parts of the high plateau; the beaver only in Lake Zeribar, near Sulefmaniyeh.

The Iranian wild ass differs in some respects from the Mesopotamian. His skin is smooth, like that of a deer, and of a reddish color, the belly and hinder parts partaking of a silvery gray; his head and ears are large and somewhat clumsy; but his neck is fine, and his legs are beautifully slender. His mane is short and black, and he has a black tuft at the end of his tail, but no dark line runs along his back or crosses his shoulders. The Persians call him the gur-khur, and chase him with occasional success, regarding his flesh as a great delicacy. He appears to be the Asinus onager of naturalists, a distinct species from the Asinus hemippus of Mesopotamia, and the Asinus hemionus of Thibet and Tartary.

It is doubtful whether some kind of wild cattle does not still inhabit the more remote tracts of Kurdistan. The natives mention among the animals of their country "the mountain ox;" and though it has been suggested that the beast intended is the elk, it is perhaps as likely to be the Aurochs, which seems certainly to have been a native of the adjacent country of Mesopotamia in ancient times. At any rate, until Zagros has been thoroughly explored by Europeans, it must remain uncertain what animal is meant. Meanwhile we may be tolerably sure that, besides the species enumerated, Mount Zagros contains within its folds some large and rare ruminant.

Among the birds the most remarkable are the eagle, the bustard, the pelican, the stork, the pheasant, several kinds of partridges, the quail, the woodpecker, the bee-eater, the hoopoe, and the nightingale. Besides these, doves and pigeons, both wild and tame, are common; as are swallows, goldfinches, sparrows, larks, blackbirds, thrushes, linnets, magpies, crows, hawks, falcons, teal, snipe, wild ducks, and many other kinds of waterfowl. The most common partridge is a red-legged species (Caccabis chukar of naturalists), which is unable to fly far, and is hunted until it drops. Another kind, common both in Azerbijan and in the Elburz, is the black-breasted partridge (Perdix nigra)—a bird not known in many countries. Besides these, there is a small gray partridge in the Zagros range, which the Kurds call seslca. The bee-eater (Merops Persicus) is rare. It is a bird of passage, and only visits Media in the autumn, preparatory to retreating into the warm district of Mazandoran for the winter months. The hoopoe (Upupa) is probably still rarer, since very few travellers mention it. The woodpecker is found in Zagros, and is a beautiful bird, red and gray in color.

Media is, on the whole, but scantily provided with fish. Lake Urumiyeh produces none, as its waters are so salt that they even destroy all the river-fish which enter them. Salt streams, like the Aji Su, are equally unproductive, and the fresh-water rivers of the plateau fall so low in summer that fish cannot become numerous in them. Thus it is only in Zagros, in Azerbijan, and in the Elburz, that the streams furnish any considerable quantity. The kinds most common are barbel, carp, dace, bleak, and gudgeon. In a comparatively few streams, more especially those of Zagros, trout are found, which are handsome and of excellent quality. The river of Isfahan produces a kind of crayfish, which is taken in the bushes along its banks, and is very delicate eating.

It is remarkable that fish are caught not only in the open streams of Media, but also in the kanats or underground conduits, from which the light of day is very nearly excluded. They appear to be of one sort only, viz., barbel, but are abundant, and often grow to a considerable size. Chardin supposed them to be unfit for food; but a later observer declares that, though of no great delicacy, they are "perfectly sweet and wholesome."

Of reptiles, the most common are snakes, lizards, and tortoises. In the long grass of the Moghan district, on the lower course of the Araxes, the snakes are so numerous and venomous that many parts of the plain are thereby rendered impassable in the summer-time. A similar abundance of this reptile near the western entrance of the Girduni Siyaluk pass induces the natives to abstain from using it except in winter. Lizards of many forms and hues disport themselves about the rocks and stones, some quite small, others two feet or more in length. They are quite harmless, and appear to be in general very tame. Land tortoises are also common in the sandy regions. In Kurdistan there is a remarkable frog, with a smooth skin and of an apple-green color, which lives chiefly in trees, roosting in them at night, and during the day employing itself in catching flies and locusts, which it strikes with its fore paw, as a cat strikes a bird or a mouse.

Among insects, travellers chiefly notice the mosquito, which is in many places a cruel torment; the centipede, which grows to an unusual size; the locust, of which there is more than one variety; and the scorpion, whose sting is sometimes fatal.

The destructive locust (the Acridium peregrinum, probably) comes suddenly into Kurdistan and southern Media in clouds that obscure the air, moving with a slow and steady flight and with a sound like that of heavy rain, and settling in myriads on the fields, the gardens, the trees, the terraces of the houses, and even the streets, which they sometimes cover completely. Where they fall, vegetation presently disappears; the leaves, and even the stems of the plants, are devoured; the labors of the husbandman through many a weary month perish in a day; and the curse of famine is brought upon the land which but now enjoyed the prospect of an abundant harvest. It is true that the devourers are themselves devoured to some extent by the poorer sort of people; but the compensation is slight and temporary; in a few days, when all verdure is gone, either the swarms move to fresh pastures, or they perish and cover the fields with their dead bodies, while the desolation which they have created continues. [PLATE III., Fig. 2.]

Another kind of locust, observed by Mr. Rich in Kurdistan, is called by the natives shira-kulla, a name seemingly identical with the chargol of the Jews, and perhaps the best clue which we possess to the identification of that species. Mr. Rich describes it as "a large insect, about four inches long, with no wings, but a kind of sword projecting from the tail. It bites," he says, "pretty severely, but does no harm to the cultivation." We may recognize in this description a variety of the great green grasshopper (Locusta viridissima), many species of which are destitute of wings, or have wing-covers only, and those of a very small size.

The scorpion of the country (Scorpio crassicauda) has been represented as peculiarly venomous, more especially that which abounds in the city and neighborhood of Kashan; but the most judicious observers deny that there is any difference between the Kashan scorpion and that of other parts of the plateau, while at the same time they maintain that if the sting be properly treated, no danger need be apprehended from it. The scorpion infests houses, hiding itself under cushions and coverlets, and stings the moment it is pressed upon; some caution is thus requisite in avoiding it; but it hurts no one unless molested, and many Europeans have resided for years in the country without having ever been stung by it. [PLATE III., Fig. 3.]

The domestic animals existing at present within the limits of the ancient Media are the camel, the horse, the mule, the ass, the cow, the goat, the sheep, the dog, the cat, and the buffalo. The camel is the ordinary beast of burden in the flat country, and can carry an enormous weight. Three kinds are employed—the Bactrian or two-humped camel, which is coarse and low; the taller and lighter Arabian breed; and a cross between the two, which is called ner, and is valued very highly. The ordinary burden of the Arabian camel is from seven to eight hundredweight; while the Bactrian variety is said to be capable of bearing a load nearly twice as heavy.

Next to the camel, as a beast of burden, must be placed the mule the mules of the country are small, but finely proportioned, and carry a considerable weight. They travel thirty miles a day with ease, and are preferred for journeys on which it is necessary to cross the mountains. The ass is very inferior, and is only used by the poorer classes.

Fig 1

Pigeon towers near Isfahan.

Fig. 2.,

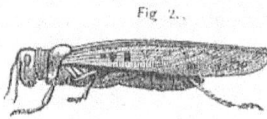

The destructive Locust (*Acridium peregrinum*).

Fig. 3.

The Scorpion (*Scorpio crassicauda*).

Fig. 4

Persepolitan horse, perhaps Nisæan.

PLATE III

Two distinct breeds of horses are now found in Media, both of which seem to be foreign—the Turkoman and the Arabian. The Turkoman is a large, powerful, enduring animal, with long legs, a light body, and a big head. The Arab is much smaller, but perfectly shaped, and sometimes not greatly inferior to the very best produce of Nejd. A third breed is obtained by an intermixture of those two, which is called the bid-pai, or "wind footed," and is the most prized of all.

The dogs are of various breeds, but the most esteemed is a large kind of gray hound, which some suppose to have been introduced into this part of Asia by the Macedonians, and which is chiefly employed in the chase of the antelope. The animal is about the height of a full sized English grayhound, but rather stouter; he is deep-chested, has long, smooth hair, and the tail considerably feathered. His pace is inferior to that of our grayhounds, but in strength and sagacity he far surpasses them.

We do not find many of the products of Media celebrated by ancient writers. Of its animals, those which had the highest reputation were its horses, distinguished into two breeds, an ordinary kind, of which Media produced annually many thousands, and a kind of rare size and excellence, known under the name of Nisaean. These last are celebrated by Herodotus, Strabo, Arrian, Ammianus Marcellinus, Suidas, and others. They are said to have been of a peculiar shape; and they were equally famous for size, speed, and stoutness. Strabo remarks that they resemble the horses known in his own time as Parthian; and this observation seems distinctly to connect them with the Turkoman breed mentioned above, which is derived exactly from the old Parthian country. In color they were often, if not always, white. We have no representation on the monuments which we can regard as certainly intended for a Nissean horse, but perhaps the figure from Persepolis may be a Persian sketch of the animal. [PLATE III., Fig. 4.]

The mules and small cattle (sheep and goats) were in sufficient repute to be required, together with horses, in the annual tribute paid to the Persian king.

Of vegetable products assigned to Media by ancient writers, the most remarkable is the "Median apple," or citron. Pliny says it was the sole tree for which Media was famous, and that it would only grow there and in Persia. Theophrastus, Dioscorides, Virgil, and other writers, celebrate its wonderful qualities, distinctly assigning it to the same region. The citron, however, will not grow in the country which has been here termed Media. It flourishes only in the warm tract between Shiraz and the Persian Gulf, and in the low sheltered region, south of the Caspian, the modern Ghilan and Mazanderan. No doubt it was the inclusion of this latter region within the limits of Media by many of the later geographers that gave to this product of the Caspian country an appellation which is really a misnomer.

Another product whereto Media gave name, and probably with more reason, was a kind of clover or lucerne, which was said to have been introduced into Greece by the Persians in the reign of Darius, and which was afterwards cultivated largely in Italy. Strabo considers this plant to have been the chief food of the Median horses, while Dioscorides assigns it certain medicinal qualities. Clover is still cultivated, in the Elburz region, but horses are now fed almost entirely on straw and barley.

Media was also famous for its silphium, or assafoetida, a plant which the country still produces, though not in any large quantity. No drug was in higher repute with the ancients for medicinal purposes; and though the Median variety was a coarse kind, inferior in repute, not only to the Cyrenaic, but also to the Parthian and the Syrian, it seems to have been exported both to Greece and Borne, and to have been largely used by druggists, however little esteemed by physicians.

The other vegetable products which Media furnished, or was believed to furnish, to the ancient world, were bdellium, amomum, cardamomum, gum tragacanth, wild-vine oil, and sagaponum, or the Ferula persica. Of these, gum tragacanth is still largely produced, and is an important article of commerce. Wild vines abound in Zagros and Elburz, but no oil is at present made from them. Bdellium, if it is benzoin, amomum, and cardamomum were perhaps rather imported through Media than the actual produce of the country, which is too cold in the winter to grow any good spices.

The mineral products of Media noted by the ancient writers are nitre, salt, and certain gems, as emeralds, lapis lazuli, and the following obscurer kinds, the zathene, the gassinades, and the narcissitis. The nitre of Media is noticed by Pliny, who says it was procured in small quantities, and was called "halmyraga." It was found in certain dry-looking glens, where the ground was white with it, and was obtained there purer than in other places. Saltpetre is still derived from the Elburz range, and also from Azerbijan.

The salt of Lake Urumiyeh is mentioned by Strabo, who says that it forms naturally on the surface, which would imply a far more complete saturation of the water than at present exists, even in the driest seasons. The gems above mentioned are assigned to Media chiefly by Pliny. The Median emeralds, according to him, were of the largest size; they varied considerably, sometimes approaching to the character of the sapphire, in which case they were apt to be veiny, and to have flaws in them. They were far less esteemed than the emeralds of many other countries. The Median lapis lazuli, on the other hand, was the best of its kind. It was of three colors—light blue, dark blue, and purple. The golden specks, however, with which it was sprinkled—really spots of yellow pyrites—rendered it useless to the gem-engravers of Pliny's time. The zathene, the gassinades, and the narcissitis were gems of inferior value. As they have not yet been identified with any known species, it will be unnecessary to prolong the present chapter by a consideration of them.

CHAPTER III

CHARACTER, MANNERS AND CUSTOMS, ARTS, ETC., OF THE PEOPLE

"Pugnatrix natio et formidanda."—Amm. Marc, xxiii. 6.

The ethnic character of the Median people is at the present day scarcely a matter of doubt. The close connection which all history, sacred and profane, establishes between them and the Persians, the evidence of their proper names and of their language, so far as it is known to us, together with the express statements of Herodotus and Strabo, combine to prove that they belonged to that branch of the human family known to us as the Arian or Iranic, a leading subdivision of the great Indo-European race. The tie of a common language, common manners and customs, and to a great extent a common belief, united in ancient times all the dominant tribes of the great plateau, extending even beyond the plateau in one direction to the Jaxartes (Syhun) and in another to the Hyphasis (Sutlej). Persians, Medes, Sagartians, Chorasmians, Bactrians, Sogdians, Hyrcanians, Sarangians, Gandarians, and Sanskritic Indians belonged all to a single stock, differing from one another probably not much more than now differ the various subdivisions of the Teutonic or the Slavonic race. Between the tribes at the two extremities of the Arian territory the divergence was no doubt considerable; but between any two neighboring tribes the difference was probably in most cases exceedingly slight. At any rate this was the case towards the west, where the Medes and Persians, the two principal sections of the Arian body in that quarter, are scarcely distinguishable from one another in any of the features which constitute ethnic type.

The general physical character of the ancient Arian race is best gathered from the sculptures of the Achsemenian kings, which exhibit to us a very noble variety of the human species—a form tall, graceful, and stately; a physiognomy handsome and pleasing, often somewhat resembling the Greek; the forehead high and straight, the nose nearly in the same line, long and well formed, sometimes markedly aquiline, the upper lip short, commonly shaded by a moustache, the chin rounded and generally covered with a curly beard. The hair evidently grew in great plenty, and the race was proud of it. On the top of the head it was worn smooth, but it was drawn back from the forehead and twisted into a row or two of crisp curls, while at the same time it was arranged into a large mass of similar small close ringlets at the back of the head and over the ears. [PLATE IV., Fig. 1.]

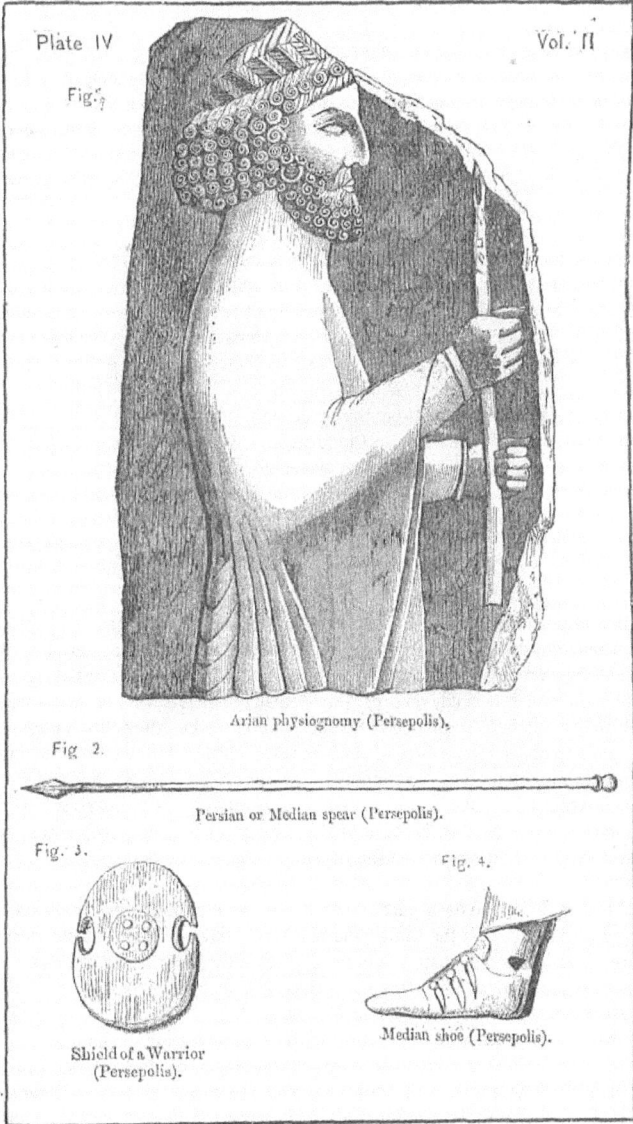

Plate IV

Vol. II

Fig. 1

Arian physiognomy (Persepolis).

Fig 2.

Persian or Median spear (Persepolis).

Fig. 3.

Fig. 4.

Shield of a Warrior (Persepolis).

Median shoe (Persepolis).

PLATE IV

Of the Median women we have no representations upon the sculptures; but we are informed by Xenophon that they were remarkable for their stature and their beauty. The same qualities were observable in the women of Persia, as we learn from Plutarch, Ammianus Marcellinus, and others. The Arian races seem in old times to have treated women with a certain chivalry, which allowed the full development of their physical powers, and rendered them specially attractive alike to their own husbands and to the men of other nations.

The modern Persian is a very degenerate representative of the ancient Arian stock. Slight and supple in person, with quick, glancing eyes, delicate features, and a vivacious manner, he lacks the dignity and strength, the calm repose and simple grace of the race from which he is sprung, Fourteen centuries of subjection to despotic sway have left their stamp upon his countenance and his frame, which, though still retaining some traces of the original type, have been sadly weakened and lowered by so long a term of subservience. Probably the wild Kurd or Lur of the present day more nearly corresponds in physique to the ancient Mede than do the softer inhabitants of the great plateau.

Among the moral characteristics of the Medes the one most obvious is their bravery. "Pugnatrix natio et formidanda," says Ammianus Marcellinus in the fourth century of our era, summing up in a few words the general judgment of Antiquity. Originally equal, if not superior, to their close kindred, the Persians, they were throughout the whole period of Persian supremacy only second to them in courage and warlike qualities. Mardonius, when allowed to take his choice out of the entire host of Xerxes, selected the Median troops in immediate succession to the Persians. Similarly, when the time for battle came he kept the Medes near himself, giving them their place in the line close to that of the Persian contingent. It was no doubt on account of their valor, as Diodorus suggests, that the Medes were chosen to make the first attack upon the Greek position at Thermopylae, where, though unsuccessful, they evidently showed abundant courage. In the earlier times, before riches and luxury had eaten out the strength of the race, their valor and military prowess must have been even more conspicuous. It was then especially that Media deserved to be called, as she is in Scripture, "the mighty one of the heathen"—"the terrible of the nations."

Her valor, undoubtedly, was of the merciless kind. There was no tenderness, no hesitancy about it. Not only did her armies "dash to pieces" the fighting men of the nations opposed to her, allowing apparently no quarter, but the women and the children suffered indignities and cruelties at the hands of her savage warriors, which the pen unwillingly records. The Median conquests were accompanied by the worst atrocities which lust and hate combined are wont to commit when they obtain their full swing. Neither the virtue of women nor the innocence of children were a protection to them. The infant was slain before the very eye of the parent. The sanctity of the hearth was invaded, and the matron ravished beneath her own roof-tree. Spoil, it would seem, was disregarded in comparison with insult and vengeance; and the brutal soldiery cared little either for silver or gold, provided they could indulge freely in that thirst for blood which man shares with the hyena and the tiger.

The habits of the Medes in the early part of their career were undoubtedly simple and manly. It has been observed with justice that the same general features have at all times distinguished the rise and fall of Oriental kingdoms and dynasties. A brave and adventurous prince, at the head of a population at once poor, warlike, and greedy, overruns a vast tract, and acquires extensive dominion, while his successors, abandoning themselves to sensuality and sloth, probably also to oppressive and irascible dispositions, become in process of time victims to those same qualities in another prince and people which had enabled their own predecessor to establish their power. It was as being braver, simpler, and so stronger than the Assyrians that the Medes were able to dispossess them of their sovereignty over western Asia. But in this, as in most other cases of conquest throughout the East, success was followed almost immediately by degeneracy. As captive Greece captured her fierce conqueror, so the subdued

Assyrians began at once to corrupt their subduers. Without condescending to a close imitation of Assyrian manners and customs, the Medes proceeded directly after their conquest to relax the severity of their old habits and to indulge in the delights of soft and luxurious living. The historical romance of Xenophon presents us probably with a true picture when it describes the strong contrast which existed towards the close of the Median period between the luxury and magnificence which prevailed at Ecbatana, and the primitive simplicity of Persia Proper, where the old Arian habits, which had once been common to the two races, were still maintained in all their original severity. Xenophon's authority in this work is, it must be admitted, weak, and little trust can be placed in the historical accuracy of his details; but his general statement is both in itself probable, and is also borne out to a considerable extent by other authors. Herodotus and Strabo note the luxury of the Median dress, while the latter author goes so far as to derive the whole of the later Persian splendor from an imitation of Median practices. We must hold then that towards the latter part of their empire the Medes became a comparatively luxurious people, not indeed laying aside altogether their manly habits, nor ceasing to be both brave men and good soldiers, but adopting an amount of pomp and magnificence to which they were previously strangers, affecting splendor in their dress and apparel, grandeur and rich ornament in their buildings, variety in their banquets, and attaining on the whole a degree of civilization not very greatly inferior to that of the Assyrians. In taste and real refinement they seem indeed to have fallen considerably below their teachers. A barbaric magnificence predominated in their ornamentation over artistic effort, richness in the material being preferred to skill in the manipulation. Literature, and even letters, were very sparingly cultivated. But little originality was developed. A stately dress, and a new style of architecture, are almost the only inventions to which the Medes can lay claim. They were brave, energetic, enterprising, fond of display, capable of appreciating to some extent the advantages of civilized life; but they had little genius, and the world is scarcely indebted to them for a single important addition to the general stock of its ideas.

Of the Median customs in war we know but little. Herodotus tells us that in the army of Xerxes the Medes were armed exactly as the Persians, carrying on their heads a soft felt cap, on their bodies a sleeved tunic, and on their legs trousers. Their offensive arms, he says, were the spear, the bow, and the dagger. They had large wicker shields, and bore their quivers suspended at their backs. Sometimes their tunic was made into a coat of mail by the addition to it on the outside of a number of small iron plates arranged so as to overlap each other, like the scales of a fish. They served both on horseback and on foot, with the same equipment in both cases.

There is no reason to doubt the correctness of this description of the Median military dress under the early Persian kings. The only question is how far the equipment was really the ancient warlike custom of the people. It seems in some respects too elaborate to be the armature of a simple and primitive race. We may reasonably suppose that at least the scale armor and the unwieldy wicker shields (yeppa), which required to be rested on the ground, were adopted at a somewhat late date from the Assyrians. At any rate the original character of the Median armies, as set before us in Scripture, and as indicated both by Strabo and Xenophon, is simpler than the Herodotean description. The primitive Modes seem to have been a nation of horse-archers. Trained from their early boyhood to a variety of equestrian exercises, and well practised in the use of the bow, they appear to have proceeded against their enemies with clouds of horse, almost in Scythian fashion, and to have gained their victories chiefly by the skill with which they shot their arrows as they advanced, retreated, or manoeuvred about their foe. No doubt they also used the sword and the spear. The employment of these weapons has been almost universal throughout the East from a very remote antiquity, and there is some mention of them in connection with the Medes and their kindred, the Persians, in Scripture; but it is evident that the terror which the Medes inspired arose mainly from their dexterity as archers.

No representation of weapons which can be distinctly recognized as Median has come down to us. The general character of the military dress and of the arms appears, probably in the Persepolitan sculptures;

but as these reliefs are in most cases representations, not of Medes, but of Persians, and as they must be hereafter adduced in illustration of the military customs of the latter people, only a very sparing use of them can be made in the present chapter. It would seem that the bow employed was short, and very much curved, and that, like the Assyrian it was usually carried in a bow-case, which might either be slung at the back, or hung from the girdle. [PLATE V., Fig. 1.] The arrows, which were borne in a quiver slung behind the right shoulder, must have been short, certainly not exceeding the length of three feet. The quiver appears to have been round; it was covered at the top, and was fastened by means of a flap and strap, which last passed over, a button. [PLATE V. Fig. 1.] The Median spear or lance was from six to seven feet in length. Its head was lozenge-shaped and flattish, but strengthened by a bar or line down the middle. It is uncertain whether the head was inserted into the top of the shaft, or whether it did not rather terminate in a ring or socket into which the upper end of the shaft was itself inserted. The shaft tapered gradually from bottom to top, and terminated below in a knob or ball, which was perhaps sometimes carved into the shape of some natural object. [PLATE IV., Fig. 2.]

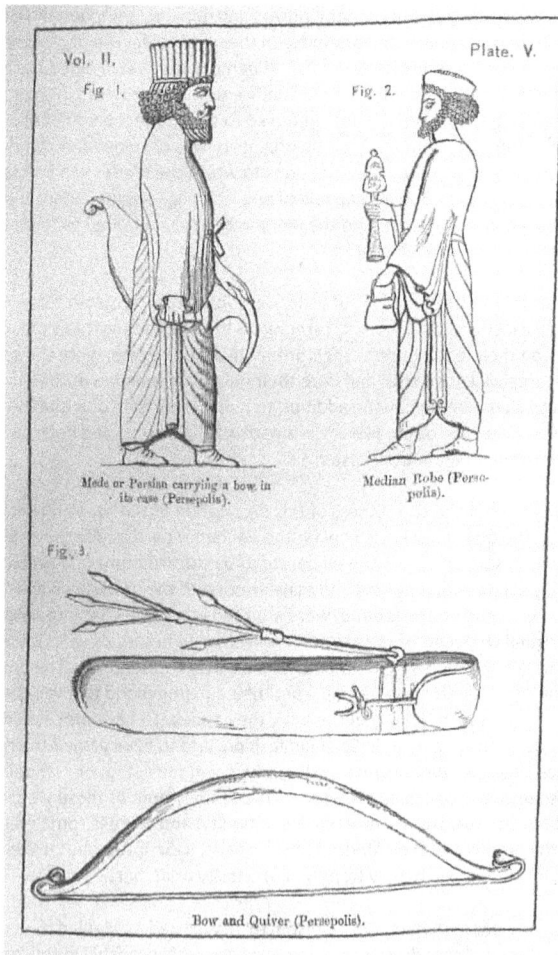

Vol. II,

Fig 1.

Plate. V.

Fig. 2.

Mede or Persian carrying a bow in its case (Persepolis).

Median Robe (Persepolis).

Fig. 3.

Bow and Quiver (Persepolis).

PLATE V

The sword was short, being in fact little more than a dagger. It depended at the right thigh from a belt which encircled the waist, and was further secured by a strap attached to the bottom of the sheath, and passing round the soldier's right leg a little above the knee.

Median shields were probably either round or oval. The oval specimens bore a resemblance to the shield of the Boeotians, having a small oval aperture at either side, apparently for the sake of greater lightness. They were strengthened at the centre by a circular boss or disk, ornamented with knobs or circles. They would seem to have been made either of metal or wood. [PLATE IV., Fig. 3.]

The favorite dress of the Medes in peace is well known to us from the sculptures; there can be no reasonable doubt that the long flowing robe so remarkable for its graceful folds, which is the garb of the kings, the chief nobles, and the officers of the court in all the Persian bas-reliefs, and which is seen also upon the darics and the gems, is the famous "Median garment" of Herodotus, Xenophon, and Strabo. [PLATE V., Fig. 2.] This garment fits the chest and shoulders closely, but falls over the arms in two large loose sleeves, open at the bottom. At the waist it is confined by a cincture. Below it is remarkably full and ample, drooping in two clusters of perpendicular folds at the two sides, and between these hanging in festoons like a curtain. It extends down to the ankles, where it is met by a high shoe or low boot, opening in front, and secured by buttons. [PLATE IV., Fig. 4.]

These Median robes were of many colors. Sometimes they were purple, sometimes scarlet, occasionally a dark gray, or a deep crimson. Procopius says that they were made of silk, and this statement is confirmed to some extent by Justin, who speaks of their transparency. It may be doubted, however, whether the material was always the same; probably it varied with the season, and also with the wealth of the wearer.

Besides this upper robe, which is the only garment shown in the sculptures, the Medes wore as under garments a sleeved shirt or tunic of a purple color, and embroidered drawers or trousers. They covered the head, not only out of doors, but in their houses, wearing either felt caps like the Persians, or a head-dress of a more elaborate character, which bore the name of tiara or cidaris. This appears to have been, not a turban, but rather a kind of high-crowned hat, either stiff or flexible, made probably of felt or cloth, and dyed of different hues, according to the fancy of the owner. [PLATE VI., Fig. 1.]

The Medes took a particular delight in the ornamentation of their persons. According to Xenophon, they were acquainted with most of the expedients by the help of which vanity attempts to conceal the ravages of time and to create an artificial beauty. They employed cosmetics, which they rubbed into the skin, for the sake of improving the complexion. They made use of an abundance of false hair. Like many other Oriental nations, both ancient and modern, they applied dyes to enhance the brilliancy of the eyes, and give them a greater apparent size and softness. They were also fond of wearing golden ornaments. Chains or collars of gold usually adorned their nocks, bracelets of the same precious metal encircled their wrists, and earrings were inserted into their ears. [PLATE VI., Fig. 2.] Gold was also used in the caparisons of their horses, the bit and other parts of the harness being often of this valuable material.

We are told that the Medes were very luxurious at their banquets. Besides plain meat and game of different kinds, with the ordinary accompaniments of wine and bread, they were accustomed to place before their guests a vast number of side-dishes, together with a great variety of sauces. They ate with the hand, as is still the fashion in the East, and were sufficiently refined to make use of napkins. Each guest had his own dishes, and it was a mark of special honor to augment their number. Wine was drunk both at the meal and afterwards, often in an undue quantity; and the close of the feast was apt to be a scene of general turmoil and confusion. At the Court it was customary for the king to receive his wine at the hands of a cupbearer, who first tasted the draught, that the king might be sure that it was not poisoned, and then presented it to his master with much pomp and ceremony.

The whole ceremonial of the court seems to have been imposing. Under ordinary circumstances the monarch kept himself secluded, and no one could obtain admission to him unless he formally requested an audience, and was introduced into the royal presence by the proper officer. On his admission he prostrated himself upon the ground with the same signs of adoration which were made on entering a temple. The king, surrounded by his attendants, eunuchs, and others, maintained a haughty reserve, and the stranger only beheld him from a distance. Business was transacted in a great measure by writing. The monarch rarely quitted his palace, contenting himself with such reports of the state of his empire as were transmitted to him from time to time by his officers.

The chief amusement of the court, in which however the king rarely partook, was hunting. Media always abounded in beasts of chase; and lions, bears, leopards, wild boars, stags, gazelles, wild sheep, and wild asses are mentioned among the animals hunted by the Median nobles. Of these the first four were reckoned dangerous, the others harmless. It was customary to pursue these animals on horseback, and to aim at them with the bow or the javelin. We may gather a lively idea of some of these hunts from the sculptures of the Parthians, who some centuries later inhabited the same region. We see in these the rush of great troops of boars through marshes dense with water-plants, the bands of beaters urging them on, the sportsmen aiming at them with their bows, and the game falling transfixed with two or three well-aimed shafts. Again we see herds of deer driven within enclosures, and there slain by archers who shoot from horseback, the monarch under his parasol looking on the while, pleased with the dexterity of his servants. It is thus exactly that Xenophon portrays Astyages as contemplating the sport of his courtiers, complacently viewing their enjoyment, but taking no active part in the work himself.

Like other Oriental sovereigns, the Median monarch maintained a seraglio of wives and concubines; and polygamy was commonly practised among the more wealthy classes. Strabo speaks of a strange law as obtaining with some of the Median tribes—a law which required that no man should be content with fewer wives than five. It is very unlikely that such a burden was really made obligatory on any: most probably five legitimate wives, and no more, were allowed by the law referred to, just as four wives, and no more, are lawful for Mohammedans. Polygamy, as usual, brought in its train the cruel practice of castration; and the court swarmed with eunuchs, chiefly foreigners purchased in their infancy. Towards the close of the Empire this despicable class appears to have been all-powerful with the monarch.

Thus the tide of corruption gradually advanced; and there is reason to believe that both court and people had in a great measure laid aside the hardy and simple customs of their forefathers, and become enervated through luxury, when the revolt of the Persians came to test the quality of their courage, and their ability to maintain their empire. It would be improper in this place to anticipate the account of this struggle, which must be reserved for the historical chapter; but the well-known result—the speedy and complete success of the Persians—must be adduced among the proofs of a rapid deterioration in the Median character between the accession of Cyaxares and the capture—less than a century later—of Astyages.

We have but little information with respect to the state of the arts among the Medes. A barbaric magnificence characterized, as has been already observed, their architecture, which differed from the Assyrian in being dependent for its effect on groups of pillars rather than on painting or sculpture. Still sculpture was, it is probable, practised to some extent by the Medes, who, it is almost certain, conveyed on to the Persians those modifications of Assyrian types which meet us everywhere in the remains of the Achsemenian monarch? The carving of winged genii, of massive forms of bulls and lions, of various grotesque monsters, and of certain clumsy representations of actual life, imitated from the bas-reliefs of the Assyrians, may be safely ascribed to the Medes; since, had they not carried on the traditions of their predecessors, Persian art could not have borne the resemblance that it does to Assyrian. But these first mimetic efforts of the Arian race have almost wholly perished, and there scarcely seems to remain more than a single fragment which can be assigned on even plausible grounds to the Median period. A portion of a colossal lion, greatly injured by time, is still to be seen at Hamadan, the site of the great Median capital, which the best judges regard as anterior to the Persian period, and as therefore most probably Median. It consists of the head and body of the animal, from which the four legs and the tail have been broken off, and measures between eleven and twelve feet from the crown of the head to the point from which the tail sprang. By the position of the head and what remains of the shoulders and thighs, it is evident that the animal was represented in a sitting posture, with the fore legs straight and the hind legs gathered up under it. To judge of the feeling and general character of the sculpture is difficult, owing to the worn and mutilated condition of the work; but we seem to trace in it the same air of calm and serene majesty that characterizes the colossal bulls and lions of Assyria, together with somewhat more of expression and of softness than are seen in the productions of that people. Its posture, which is unlike that of any Assyrian specimen, indicates a certain amount of originality as belonging to the Median artists, while its colossal size seems to show that the effect on the spectator was still to be produced, not so much by expression, finish, or truth to nature, as by mere grandeur of dimension. [PLATE VI., Fig. 3.]

CHAPTER IV

RELIGION

The earliest form of the Median religion is to be found in those sections of the Zendavesta which have been pronounced on internal evidence to be the most ancient portions of that venerable compilation; as, for instance, the first Fargard of the Vendidad, and the Gathas, or "Songs," which occur here and there in the Yacna, or Book on Sacrifice. In the Gathas, which belong to a very remote era indeed, we seem to have the first beginnings of the Religion. We may indeed go back by their aid to a time anterior to themselves—a time when the Arian race was not yet separated into two branches, and the Easterns and Westerns, the Indians and Iranians, had not yet adopted the conflicting creeds of Zoroastrianism and Brahminism. At that remote period we seem to see prevailing a polytheistic nature-worship—a recognition of various divine beings, called indifferently Asuras (Ahuras) or Devas, each independent of the rest, and all seemingly nature-powers rather than persons, whereof the chief are Indra, Storm or Thunder; Mithra, Sunlight; Aramati (Armaiti), Earth; Vayu, Wind; Agni, Fire; and Soma (Homa), Intoxication. Worship is conducted by priests, who are called kavi, "seers;" karapani, "sacriflcers," or ricikhs, "wise men." It consists of hymns in honor of the gods; sacrifices, bloody and unbloody, some' portion of which is burnt upon an altar; and a peculiar ceremony, called that of Soma, in which an intoxicating liquor is offered to the gods, and then consumed by the priests, who drink till they are drunken.

Such, in outline, is the earliest phase of Arian religion, and it is common to both branches of the stock, and anterior to the rise of the Iranic, Median, or Persian system. That system is a revolt from this sensuous and superficial nature-worship. It begins with a distinct recognition of spiritual intelligences—real persons—with whom alone, and not with powers, religion is concerned. It divides these intelligences into good and bad, pure and impure, benignant and malevolent. To the former it applies the term Asuras (Ahuras), "living" or "spiritual beings," in a good sense; to the latter, the term Devas, in a bad one. It regards the "powers" hitherto worshipped as chiefly Devas; but it excepts from this unfavorable view a certain number, and, recognizing them as Asuras, places them above the Izeds, or "angels." Thus far it has made two advances, each of great importance, the substitution of real "persons" for "powers," as objects of the religious faculty, and the separation of the persons into good and bad, pure and impure, righteous and wicked. But it does not stop here. It proceeds to assert, in a certain sense, monotheism against polytheism. It boldly declares that, at the head of the good intelligences, is a single great Intelligence, Ahuro-Mazdao, the highest object of adoration, the true Creator, Preserver, and Governor of the universe. This is its great glory. It sets before the soul a single Being as the source of all good and the proper object of the highest worship. Ahuro-Mazdao is "the creator of life, the earthly and the spiritual;" "he has made the celestial bodies, earth, water, and trees, all good creatures," and "all good, true, holy, pure, things." He is "the Holy God, the Holiest, the essence of truth, the father of all truth, the best being of all, the master of purity." He is supremely "happy," possessing every blessing, "health, wealth, virtue, wisdom, immortality." From him comes all good to man; on the pious and the righteous he bestows not only earthly advantages, but precious spiritual gifts, truth, devotion, "the good mind," and everlasting happiness; and as he rewards the good, so he punishes the bad, though this is an aspect in which he is but seldom represented.

It has been said that this conception of Ahura-mazda as the Supreme Being is "perfectly identical with the notion of Elohim, or Jehovah, which we find in the books of the Old Testament." This is, no doubt, an over-statement. Ahura-mazda is less spiritual and less awful than Jehovah. He is less remote from the nature of man. The very ascription to him of health (haurvat) is an indication that he is conceived of as possessing a sort of physical nature. Lucidity and brilliancy are assigned to him, not (as it would seem) in a mere metaphorical sense. Again, he is so predominantly the author of good things, the source of blessing and prosperity, that he could scarcely inspire his votaries with any feeling of fear. Still, considering the general failure of unassisted reason to mount up to the true notion of a spiritual God, this doctrine of the early Arians is very remarkable; and its approximation to the truth sufficiently explains at once the favorable light in which its professors are viewed by the Jewish prophets, and the favorable opinion which they form of the Jewish system. Evidently, the Jews and Arians, when they became known to one another, recognized mutually the fact that they were worshippers of the same great Being. Hence the favor of the Persians towards the Jews, and the fidelity of the Jews towards the Persians. The Lord God of the Jews being recognized as identical with Ormazd, a sympathetic feeling united the peoples. The Jews, so impatient generally of a foreign yoke, never revolted from the Persians; and the Persians, so intolerant, for the most part, of religions other than their own, respected and protected Judaism.

The sympathy was increased by the fact that the religion of Ormazd was anti-idolatrous. In the early nature-worship idolatry had been allowed; but the Iranic system pronounced against it from the first. No images of Ahura-mazda, or of the Izeds, profaned the severe simplicity of an Iranic temple. It was only after a long lapse of ages that, in connection with a foreign worship, idolatry crept in. The old Zoroastrianism was in this respect as pure as the religion of the Jews, and thus a double bond of religious sympathy united the Hebrews and the Arians.

Under the supreme God, Ahura-mazda or Ormazd, the ancient Iranic system placed (as has been already observed) a number of angels. Some of these, as Vohu-mano, "the Good Mind;" Mazda, "the Wise" (?); and Asha, "the True," are scarcely distinguishable from attributes of the Divinity. Armaiti, however, the genius of the Earth, and Sraosha or Serosh, an angel, are very clearly and distinctly personified. Sraosha is Ormazd's messenger. He delivers revelations, shows men the paths of happiness, and brings them the blessings which Ormazd has assigned to their share. Another of his functions is to protect the true faith. He is called, in a very special sense, "the friend of Ormazd," and is employed by Ormazd not only to distribute his gifts, but also to conduct to him the souls of the faithful, when this life is over, and they enter on the celestial scene.

Armaiti is at once the genius of the Earth, and the goddess of Piety. The early Ormazd worshippers were agriculturists, and viewed the cultivation of the soil as a religious duty enjoined upon them by God. Hence they connected the notion of piety with earth culture; and it was but a step from this to make a single goddess preside over the two. It is as the angel of Earth that Armaiti has most distinctly a personal character. She is regarded as wandering from spot to spot, and laboring to convert deserts and wildernesses into fruitful fields and gardens. She has the agriculturist under her immediate protection, while she endeavors to persuade the shepherd, who persists in the nomadic life, to give up his old habits and commence the cultivation of the soil. She is of course the giver of fertility, and rewards her votaries by bestowing upon them abundant harvests. She alone causes all growth. In a certain cense she pervades the whole material creation, mankind included, in whom she is even sometimes said to "reside."

Armaiti, further "tells men the everlasting laws, which no one may abolish"—laws which she has learnt from converse with Ahura-mazda himself. She is thus naturally the second object of worship to the old Zoroastrian; and converts to the religion were required to profess their faith in her in direct succession to Ahura-mazda.

From Armaiti must be carefully distinguished the geus urva, or "soul of the earth"—a being who nearly resembles the "anima mundi" of the Greek and Roman philosophers. This spirit dwells in the earth itself, animating it as a man's soul animates his body. In old times, when man first began to plough the soil, geus urva cried aloud, thinking that his life was threatened, and implored the assistance of the archangels. They however were deaf to his entreaties (since Ormazd had decreed that there should be cultivation), and left him to bear his pains as he best could. It is to be hoped that in course of time he became callous to them, and made the discovery that mere scratches, though they may be painful, are not dangerous.

It is uncertain whether in the most ancient form of the Iranic worship the cult of Mithra was included or no. On the one hand, the fact that Mithra is common to both forms of the Arian creed—the Indian and Iranic—would induce the belief that his worship was adopted from the first by the Zoroastrians; on the other, the entire absence of all mention of Mithra from the Gathas would lead us to the conclusion that in the time when they were composed his cult had not yet begun. Perhaps we may distinguish between two forms of early Iranic worship—one that of the more intelligent and spiritual—the leaders of the secession—in whose creed Mithra had no place; the other that of the great mass of followers, a coarser and more material system, in which many points of the old religion were retained, and among them the worship of the Sun-god. This lower and more materialistic school of thought probably conveyed on into the Iranic system other points also common to the Zendavosta with the Vedas, as the recognition of Airyaman (Aryaman) as a genius presiding over marriages, of Vitraha as a very high angel, and the like.

Vayu, "the Wind," seems to have been regarded as a god from the first. He appears, not only in the later portions of the Zenda vesta, like Mithra and Aryaman, but in the Gathas themselves. His name is clearly identical with that of the Vedic Wind-god, Vayu, and is apparently a sister form to the ventus, or wind, of the more western Arians. The root is probably vi, "to go," which may be traced in vis, via, vado, venio, etc.

The ancient Iranians did not adopt into their system either Agni, "Fire" (Lat. ignis), or Soma (Homa), "Intoxication." Fire was indeed retained for sacrifice; but it was regarded as a mere material agent, and not as a mysterious Power, the proper object of prayer and worship. The Soma worship, which formed a main element of the old religion, and which was retained in Brahminism, was at the first altogether discarded by the Zoroastrians; indeed, it seems to have been one of the main causes of that disgust which split the Arian body in two, and gave rise to the new religion. A ceremony in which it was implied that the intoxication of their worshippers was pleasing to the gods, and not obscurely hinted that they themselves indulged in similar excesses, was revolting to the religious temper of those who made the Zoaroastrian reformation; and it is plain from the Gathas that the new system was intended at first to be entirely free from the pollution of so disgusting a practice. But the zeal of religious reformers outgoes in most cases the strength and patience of their people, whose spirit is too gross and earthly to keep pace with the more lofty flights of the purer and higher intelligence. The Iranian section of the Arians could not be weaned wholly from their beloved Soma feasts; and the leaders of the movement were obliged to be content ultimately with so far reforming and refining the ancient ceremony as to render it comparatively innocuous. The portion of the rite which implied that the gods themselves indulged in intoxication was omitted; and for the intoxication of the priests was substituted a moderate use of the liquor, which, instead of giving a religious sanction to drunkenness, merely implied that the Soma juice was a good gift of God, one of the many blessings for which men had to be thankful.

With respect to the evil spirits or intelligences, which, in the Zoroastrian system, stood over against the good ones, the teaching of the early reformers seems to have been less clear. The old divinities, except where adopted into the new creed, were in a general way called Devas, "fiends" or "devils," in contrast with the Ahuras, or "gods." These devas were represented as many in number, as artful, malicious, deceivers and injurers of mankind, more especially of the Zoroastrians or Ormazd-worshippers, as inventors of spells and lovers of the intoxicating Soma draught. Their leading characteristics were "destroying" and "lying." They were seldom or never called by distinct names. No account was given of their creation, nor of the origin of their wickedness. No single superior intelligence, no great Principle of Evil, was placed at their head. Ahriman (Angro-mainyus) does not occur in the Gathas as a proper name. Far less is there any graduated hierarchy of evil, surrounding a Prince of Darkness, with a sort of court, antagonistic to the angelic host of Ormazd, as in the latter portions of the Zendavesta and in the modern Parsee system.

Thus Dualism proper, or a belief in two uncreated and independent principles, one a principle of good and the other a principal of evil, was no part of the original Zoroastrianism. At the same time we find, even in the Gathas, the earliest portions of the Zondavesta, the germ out of which Dualism sprung. The contrast between good and evil is strongly and sharply marked in the Gathas; the writers continually harp upon it, their minds are evidently struck with this sad antithesis which colors the whole moral world to them; they see everywhere a struggle between right and wrong, truth and falsehood, purity and impurity; apparently they are blind to the evidence of harmony and agreement in the universe, discerning nothing anywhere but strife, conflict, antagonism. Nor is this all. They go a step further, and personify the two parties to the struggle. One is a "white" or holy "Spirit" (cpento mainyus), and the other a "dark spirit" (angro mainyus). But this personification is merely poetical or metaphorical, not real. The "white spirit" is not Ahura-mazda, and the "dark spirit" is not a hostile intelligence. Both resolve themselves on examination into mere figures of speech—phantoms of poetic imagery—abstract notions, clothed by language with an apparent, not a real, personality.

It was natural that, as time went on, Dualism should develop itself out of the primitive Zoroastrianism. Language exercises a tyranny over thought, and abstractions in the ancient world were ever becoming persons. The Iranian mind, moreover, had been strack, when it first turned to contemplate the world, with a certain antagonism; and, having once entered this track, it would be compelled to go on, and seek to discover the origin of the antagonism, the cause (or causes) to which it was to be ascribed. Evil seemed most easily accounted for by the supposition of an evil Person; and the continuance of an equal struggle, without advantage to either side, which was what the Iranians thought they beheld in the world that lay around them, appeared to them to imply the equality of that evil Person with the Being whom they rightly regarded as the author of all good. Thus Dualism had its birth. The Iranians came to believe in the existence of two co-eternal and co-equal Persons, one good and the other evil, between whom there had been from all eternity a perpetual and never-ceasing conflict, and between whom the same conflict would continue to rage through all coming time.

It is impossible to say how this development took place. We have evidence, however, that at a period considerably anterior to the commencement of the Median Empire, Dualism, not perhaps in its ultimate extravagant form, but certainly in a very decided and positive shape, had already been thought out and become the recognized creed of the Iranians. In the first Fargard, or chapter, of the Vendidad—the historical chapter, in which are traced the only movements of the Iranic peoples, and which from the geographical point whereat it stops must belong to a time when the Arians had not yet reached Media Magna—-the Dualistic belief clearly shows itself. The term Angro-mainyus has now become a proper name, and designates the great spirit of evil as definitely and determinately as Ahura-mazda designates the good spirit. The antagonism between Ahura-mazda and Angro-mainyus is depicted in the strongest colors; it is direct, constant and successful. Whatever good work Ahura-mazda in his benevolence creates, Angro-mainyus steps forward to mar and blast it. If Ahura-mazda forms a "delicious spot" in a world previously desert and uninhabitable to become the first home of his favorites, the Arians, Angro-mainyus ruins it by sending into it a poisonous serpent, and at the same time rendering the climate one of the bitterest severity. If Ahura-mazda provides, instead of this blasted region, another charming habitation, "the second best of regions and countries," Angro-mainyus sends there the curse of murrain, fatal to all cattle. To every land which Ahura-mazda creates for his worshippers, Angro-mainyus immediately assigns some plague or other. War, ravages, sickness, fever, poverty, hail, earthquakes, buzzing insects, poisonous plants, unbelief, witchcraft, and other inexpiable sins, are introduced by him into the various happy regions created without any such drawbacks by the good spirit; and a world, which should have been "very good," is by these means converted into a scene of trial and suffering.

The Dualistic principle being thus fully adopted, and the world looked on as the battle-ground between two independent and equal powers engaged in perpetual strife, it was natural that the imagination should complete the picture by ascribing to those superhuman rivals the circumstantials that accompany a great struggle between human adversaries. The two kings required, in the first place, to have their councils, which were accordingly assigned them, and were respectively composed of six councillors. The councillors of Ahura-mazda—called Amesha Spentas, or "Immortal Saints," afterwards corrupted into Amshashpands—wore Vohu-mano (Bahman), Asha-va-hista (Ardibehesht), Khshathra-vairya (Shahravar), Qpenta-Armaiti (Isfand-armat), Haurvatat (Khordad), and Ameretat (Amerdat). Those of Angro-mainyus were Ako-mano, Indra, Qaurva, Naonhaitya, and two others whose names are interpreted as "Darkness" and "Poison."

Vohu-mano (Bahman) means "the Good Mind." Originally a mere attribute of Ahura-mazda, Vohu-mano came to be considered, first as one of the high angels attendant on him, and then formally as one of-his six councillors. He had a distinct sphere or province assigned to him in Ahura-mazda's kingdom, which was the maintenance of life in animals and of goodness in man.

Asha-vahista (Ardibehesht) means "the Highest Truth"—"Voritas optima," or rather perhaps "Veritas lucidissima." He was the "Light" of the universe, subtle, all-pervading, omnipresent. His special business was to maintain the splendor of the various luminaries, and thereby to preserve all those things whose existence and growth depend on light.

Khshathra-vairya (Shahravar), whose name means simply "possessions," "wealth," was regarded as presiding over metals and as the dispenser of riches.

Qoonta-Armaiti (Isfand-armat)—the "white or holy Ar-maiti," represented the Earth. She had from the first, as we have already seen, a distinct position in the system of the Zoroastrians, where she was at once the Earth goddess and the genius of piety.

Haurvatat (Khordad) means "health"—"sanitas"—and was originally one of the great and precious gifts which Ahura-mazda possessed himself and kindly bestowed on his creatures. When personification, and the needs of the theology, had made Haurvatat an archangel, he, together with Ameretat (Amerdat),

"Immortality," took the presidency of the vegetable world, which it was the business of the pair to keep in good condition.

In the council of Angro-mainyus, Ako-mano stands in direct antithesis to Vohu-mano, as "the bad mind," or more literally, "the naught mind"—for the Zoroastrians, like Plato, regarded good and evil as identical with reality and unreality. Ako-mano's special sphere is the mind of man, where he suggests evil thoughts and prompts to bad words and wicked deeds. He holds the first place in the infernal council, as Vohu-mano does in the heavenly one.

Indra, who holds the second place in the infernal council, is evidently the Vedic god whom the Zoroastrians regarded as a powerful demon, and therefore made one of Angro-mainyus's chief councillors. He probably retained his character as the god of the storm and of war, the destroyer of crops and cities, the inspirer of armies and the wielder of the thunder-bolt. The Zoroastrians, however, ascribed to him only destructive actions; while the more logical Hindoos, observing that the same storm which hurt the crops and struck down trees and buildings was also the means of fertilizing the lands and purifying the air, viewed him under a double aspect, as at once terrible in his wrath and the bestower of numerous blessings.

Qaurva, who stands next to Indra, is thought to be the Hindoo Shiva, who has the epithet qarva in one of the Vedas. But the late appearance of Shiva in the Hindoo system makes this highly uncertain.

Naonhaitya, the fourth member of the infernal council, corresponds apparently to the Vedic Nasatyas, a collective name given to the two Aswins, the Dioscuri of Indian mythology. These were favorite gods of the early Hindoos, to whose protection they very mainly ascribed their prosperity. It was natural that the Iranians, in their aversion to their Indian brethren, should give the Aswins a seat at Angro-mainyus's council-table; but it is curious that they should represent the twin deities by only a single councillor.

Taric and Zaric, "Darkness" and "Poison," the occupants of the fifth and sixth places, are evidently personifications made for the occasion, to complete the infernal council to its full complement of six members.

As the two Principles of Good and Evil have their respective councils, so have they likewise their armies. The Good Spirit has created thousands of angelic beings, who everywhere perform his will and fight on his side against the Evil One; and the Evil One has equally on his part called into being thousands of malignant spirits who are his emissaries in the world, doing his work continually, and fighting his battles. These are the Devas or Dives, so famous in Persian fairy mythology. They are "wicked, bad, false, untrue, the originators of mischief, most baneful, destructive, the basest of all beings." The whole universe is full of them. They aim primarily at destroying all the good creations of Ahura-mazda; but if unable to destroy they content themselves with perverting and corrupting. They dog the steps of men, tempting them to sin; and, as soon as sin, obtaining a fearful power over them.

At the head of Ahura-mazda's army is the angel Sraosha (Serosh). Serosh is "the sincere, the beautiful, the victorious, the true, the master of truth." He protects the territories of the Iranians, wounds, and sometimes even slays the demons, and is engaged in a perpetual struggle against them, never slumbering night or day, but guarding the world with his drawn sword, more particularly after sunset, when the demons have the greatest power.

Angro-mainyus appears not to possess any such general-in-chief. Besides the six councillors above mentioned, there are indeed various demons of importance, as Drukhs, "destruction;" Aeshemo, "rapine;" Daivis, "deceit;" Driwis, "poverty," etc.; but no one of these seems to occupy a parallel place in the evil world to that which is assigned to Serosh in the good. Perhaps we have here a recognition of the anarchic character of evil, whose attacks are like those of a huge undisciplined host—casual, fitful, irregular—destitute wholly of that principle of law and order which gives to the resisting power of good a great portion of its efficacy.

To the belief in a spiritual world composed of all these various intelligences—one half of whom were good, and the other half evil—the early Zoroastrians added notions with respect to human duties and human prospects far more enlightened than those which have usually prevailed among heathen nations. In their system truth, purity, piety, and industry were the virtues chiefly valued and inculcated. Evil was traced up to its root in the heart of man; and it was distinctly taught that no virtue deserved the name but such as was co-extensive with the whole sphere of human activity, including the thought, as well as the word and deed. The purity required was inward as well as outward, mental as well as bodily. The industry was to be of a peculiar character. Man was placed upon the earth to preserve the good creation; and this could only be done by careful tilling of the soil, eradication of thorns and weeds, and reclamation of the tracts over which Angro-mainyus had spread the curse of barrenness. To cultivate the soil was thus a religious duty; the whole community was required to be agricultural; and either as proprietor, as farmer, or as laboring man, each Zoroastrian must "further the works of life" by advancing tillage. Piety consisted in the acknowledgment of the One True God, Ahura-mazda, and of his holy angels, the Amesha Spentas or Amshashpands, in the frequent offering of prayers, praises, and thanksgivings, in the recitation of hymns, the performance of the reformed Soma ceremony, and the occasional sacrifice of animals. Of the hymns we have abundant examples in the Gathas of the Zendavesta, and in the Yagna haptanhaiti, or "Yaana of seven chapters," which belongs to the second period of the religion. A specimen from the latter source is subjoined below. The Soma or Homa ceremony consisted in the extraction of the juice of the Homa plant by the priests during the recitation of prayers, the formal presentation of the liquid extracted to the sacrificial fire, the consumption of a small portion of it by one of the officiating priests, and the division of the remainder among the worshippers. As the juice was drunk immediately after extraction and before fermentation had set in, it was not intoxicating. The ceremony seems to have been regarded, in part, as having a mystic force, securing the favor of heaven; in part, as exerting a beneficial influence upon the body of the worshipper through the curative power inherent in the Homa plant.

The sacrifices of the Zoroastrians were never human. The ordinary victim was the horse; and we hear of occasions on which a single individual sacrificed as many as ten of these animals. Mares seem to have been regarded as the most pleasing offerings, probably on account of their superior value; and if it was desired to draw down the special favor of the Deity, those mares were selected which were already heavy in foal. Oxen, sheep, and goats were probably also used as victims. A priest always performed the sacrifice, slaying the animal, and showing the flesh to the sacred fire by way of consecration, after which it was eaten at a solemn feast by the priest and worshippers.

The Zoroastrians were devout believers in the immortality of the soul and a conscious future existence. They taught that immediately after death the souls of men, both good and bad, proceeded together along an appointed path to "the bridge of the gatherer" (chinvatperetu). This was a narrow road conducting to heaven or paradise, over which the souls of the pious alone could pass, while the wicked fell from it into the gulf below, where they found themselves in the place of punishment. The good soul was assisted across the bridge by the angel Serosh—"the happy, well-formed, swift, tall Serosh"—who met the weary wayfarer and sustained his steps as he effected the difficult passage. The prayers of his friends in this world were of much avail to the deceased, and greatly, helped him on his journey. As he entered, the archangel Vohu-mano or Bahman rose from his throne and greeted him with the words, "How happy art thou who hast come here to us from the mortality to the immortality!" Then the pious soul went joyfully onward to Ahura-mazda, to the immortal saints, to the golden throne, to Paradise. As for the wicked, when they fell into the gulf, they found themselves in outer darkness, in the kingdom of Angro-mainyus, where they were forced to remain and to feed upon poisoned banquets.

It is believed by some that the doctrine of the resurrection of the body was also part of the Zoroastrian creed. Theopompus assigned this doctrine to the Magi; and there is no reason to doubt that it was held by the priestly caste of the Arian nations in his day. We find it plainly stated in portions of the Zendavesta, which, if not among the earliest, are at any rate of very considerable antiquity, as in the eighteenth chapter of the Vendidad. It is argued that even in the Gathas there is an expression used which shows the doctrine to have been already held when they were composed; but the phrase adduced is so obscure that its true meaning must be pronounced in the highest degree uncertain. The absence of any plain allusion to the resurrection from the earlier portions of the sacred volume is a strong argument against its having formed any part of the original Arian creed—an argument which is far from outweighed by the occurrence of a more possible reference to it in a single ambiguous passage.

Around and about this nucleus of religious belief there grew up in course of time a number of legends, some of which possess considerable interest. Like other thoughtful races, the Iranians speculated upon the early condition of mankind, and conceived a golden age, and a king then reigning over a perfectly happy people, whom they called King Yima—Yima-khshaeta—the modern Persian Jemshid. Yima, according to the legend, had dwelt originally in Aryanem vaejo—the primitive seat of the Arians—and had there reigned gloriously and peacefully for awhile; but the evils of winter having come upon his country, he had removed from it with his subjects, and had retired to a secluded spot where he and his people enjoyed uninterrupted happiness. In this place was "neither overbearing nor mean-spiritedness, neither stupidity nor violence, neither poverty nor deceit, neither puniness nor deformity, neither huge teeth nor bodies beyond the usual meassure." The inhabitants suffered no defilement from the evil spirit. They dwelt amid odoriferous trees and golden pillars; their cattle were the largest, best, and most beautiful on the earth; they were themselves a tall and beautiful race; their food was ambrosial, and never failed them. No wonder that time sped fast with them, and that they, not noting its night, thought often that what was really a year had been no more than a single day. Yima was the great hero of the early Iranians. His titles, besides "the king" (khshaeta), are "the brilliant," "the happy," "the greatly wealthy," "the leader of the peoples," "the renowned in Aryanem vaejo." He is most probably identical with the Yama of the Vedas, who was originally the first man, the progenitor of mankind and the ruler of the blessed in Paradise, but who was afterwards transformed into "the god of death, the inexorable judge of men's doings, and the punisher of the wicked."

Next in importance to Yima among the heroes is Thraetona—the modern Persian Feridun. He was born in Varena—which is perhaps Atropatene, or Azerbijan—and was the son of a distinguished father, Athwyo. His chief exploit was the destruction of Ajis-dahaka (Zohak), who is sometimes represented as a cruel tyrant, the bitter enemy of the Iranian race, sometimes as a monstrous dragon, with three mouths, three tails, six eyes, and a thousand scaly rings, who threatened to ruin the whole of the good creation. The traditional scene of the destruction was the mountain of Demavend, the highest peak of the Elburz range south of the Caspian. Thraetona, like Yima, appears to be also a Vedic hero. He may be recognized in Traitana, who is said in the Rig-Veda to have slain a mighty giant by severing his head from his shoulders.

A third heroic personage known in the early times was Keresaspa, of the noble Sama family. He was the son of Thrita—a distinct personage from Thraetona—and brother of Urvakh-shaya the Just and was bred up in the arid country of Veh-keret (Khorassan). The "glory" which had rested upon Yima so many years became his in his day. He was the mightiest among the mighty, and was guarded from all danger by the fairy (pairika) Enathaiti, who followed him whithersoever he went. He slew Qravara, the queen and venomous serpent, who swallowed up men and horses. He killed Gandarewa with the golden heel, and also Cnavidhaka, who had boasted that, when he grew up, he would make the earth his wheel and heaven his chariot, that he would carry off Ahura-mazda from heaven and Angro-mainyus from hell, and yoke them both as horses to his car. Keresaspa appears as Gershasp in the modern Persian legends, where, however, but little is said of his exploits. In the Hindoo books he appears as Krigagva, the son of Samyama, and is called king of Vaigali, or Bengal!

From these specimens the general character of the early Iranic legends appears sufficiently. Without affording any very close resemblances in particular cases, they present certain general features which are common to the legendary lore of all the Western Arians. They are romantic tales, not allegories; they relate with exaggerations the deeds of men, not the processes of nature. Combining some beauty with a good deal that is bizarre and grotesque, they are lively and graphic, but somewhat childish, having in no case any deep meaning, and rarely teaching a moral lesson. In their earliest shape they appear, so far as we can judge, to have been brief, disconnected, and fragmentary. They owe the full and closely interconnected form which they assume in the Shahna-meh and other modern Persian writings, partly to a gradual accretion during the course of centuries, partly to the inventive genius of Firdausi, who wove the various and often isolated legends into a pseudo-history, and amplified them at his own pleasure. How much of the substance of Firdausi's poems belongs to really primitive myth is uncertain. We find in the Zend texts the names of Gayo-marathan, who corresponds to Kaiomars; of Haoshyanha, or Hosheng; of Yima-shaeta, or Jemshid; of Ajisdahaka, or Zohak; of Athwya, or Abtin; of Thraetona, or Feridun; of Keresaspa, or Gershasp; of Kava Uq, or Kai Kavus; of Kava Hucrava, or Kai Khosroo; and of Kava Vistaspa, or Gushtasp. But we have no mention of Tahomars; of Gava (or Gau) the blacksmith; of Feridua's sons, Selm, Tur, and Irij; of Zal, or Mino'chihr, or Eustem; of Afrasiab, or Kai Kobad; of Sohrab, or Isfendiar. And of the heroic names which actually occur in the Zendavesta, several, as Gayo-marathan, Haoshyariha, Kava Uc, and Kava Hugrava, are met with only in the later portions, which belong probably to about the fourth century before our era. The only legends which we know to be primitive are those above related, which are found in portions of the Zendavesta, whereto the best critics ascribe a high antiquity. The negative argument is not, however, conclusive; and it is quite possible that a very large proportion of Firdausi's tale may consist of ancient legends dressed up in a garb comparatively modern.

Two phases of the early Iranic religion have been now briefly described; the first a simple and highly spiritual creed, remarkable for its distinct assertion of monotheism, its hatred of idolatry, and the strongly marked antithesis which it maintained between good and evil; the second, a natural corruption of the first, Dualistic, complicated by the importance which it ascribed to angelic beings verging upon polytheism. It remains to give an account of a third phase into which the religion passed in consequence of an influence exercised upon it from without by an alien system.

When the Iranic nations, cramped for space in the countries east and south of the Caspian, began to push themselves further to the west, and then to the south, they were brought into contact with various Scythic tribes inhabiting the mountain regions of Armenia, Azerbijan, Kurdistan, and Luristan, whose religion appears to have been Magism. It was here, in these elevated tracts, where the mountains almost seem to reach the skies, that the most venerated and ancient of the fire-temples were established, some of which remain, seemingly in their primitive condition, at the present day. [PLATE VI., Fig. 4.] Here tradition placed the original seat of the fire-worship; and from hence many taught that Zoroaster, whom they regarded as the founder of Magism, had sprung. Magism was, essentially, the worship of the elements, the recognition of fire, air, earth, and water as the only proper objects of human reverence. The Magi held no personal gods, and therefore naturally rejected temples, shrines, and images, as tending to encourage the notion that gods existed of a like nature with man, i.e., possessing personality—living and intelligent beings. Theirs was a nature worship, but a nature worship of a very peculiar kind. They did not place gods over the different parts of nature, like the Greeks; they did not even personify the powers of nature, like the Hindoos; they paid their devotion to the actual material things themselves. Fire, as the most subtle and ethereal principle, and again as the most powerful agent, attracted their highest regards; and on their fire-altars the sacred flame, generally said to have been kindled from heaven, was kept burning uninterruptedly from year to year and from age to age by bands of priests, whose special duty it was to see that the sacred spark was never extinguished. To defile the altar by blowing the flame with one's breath was a capital offence; and to burn a corpse was regarded as an act equally odious. When victims were offered to fire, nothing but a small portion of the fat was consumed in the flame. Next to fire, water was reverenced. Sacrifice was offered to rivers, lakes, and fountains, the victim being brought near to them and then slain, while great care was taken that no drop of their blood should touch the water and pollute it. No refuse was allowed to be cast into a river, nor was it even lawful to wash one's hands in one. Reverence for earth was shown by sacrifice, and by abstention from the usual mode of burying the dead.

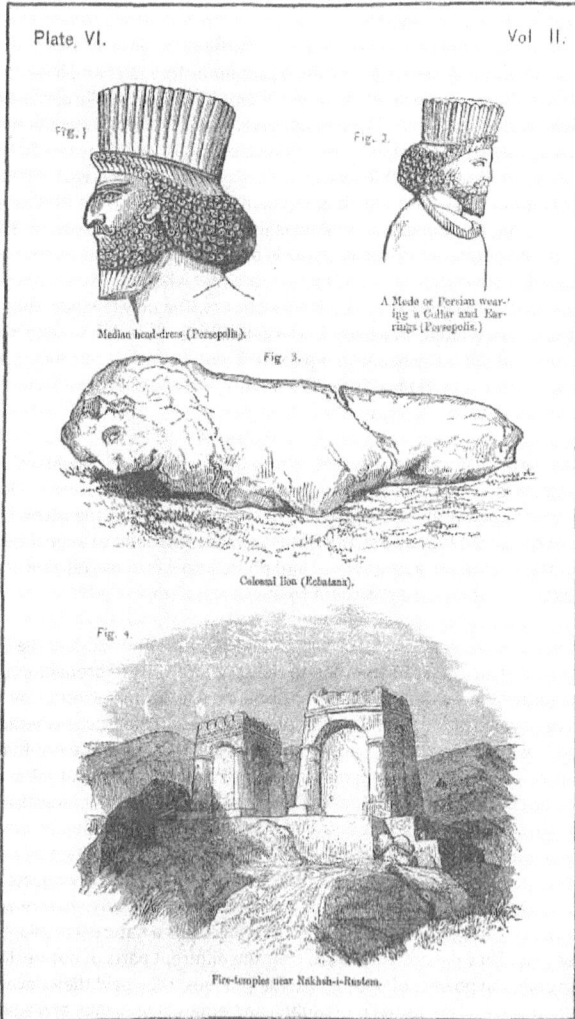

Plate. VI.   Vol II.

Fig. 1

Fig. 2

A Mede or Persian wearing a Collar and Earrings (Persepolis.)

Median head-dress (Persepolis).

Fig. 3.

Colossal lion (Ecbatana).

Fig. 4.

Fire-temples near Nakhsh-i-Rustem.

PLATE VI

The Magian religion was of a highly sacerdotal type. No worshipper could perform any religious act except by the intervention of a priest, or Magus, who stood between him and the divinity as a Mediator. The Magus prepared the victim and slew it, chanted the mystic strain which gave the sacrifice all its force, poured on the ground the propitiatory libation of oil, milk, and honey, held the bundle of thin tamarisk twigs—the Zendic barsom (baregma)—the employment of which was essential to every sacrificial ceremony. The Magi were a priest-caste, apparently holding their office by hereditary succession. They claimed to possess, not only a sacred and mediatorial character, but also supernatural prophetic powers. They explained omens, expounded dreams, and by means of a certain mysterious manipulation of the barsom, or bundle of twigs, arrived at a knowledge of future events, which they communicated to the pious inquirer.

With such pretensions it was natural that the caste should assume a lofty air, a stately dress, and an entourage of ceremonial magnificence. Clad in white robes, and bearing Upon their heads tall felt caps, with long lappets at the sides, which concealed the jaw and even the lips, each with his barsom in his hand, they marched in procession to their pynetheia, or fire altars, and standing around them performed for an hour at a time their magical incantations. The credulous multitude, impressed by sights of this kind, and imposed on by the claims to supernatural power which the Magi advanced, paid them a willing homage; the kings and chiefs consulted them; and when the Arian tribes, pressing westward, came into contact with the races professing the Magian religion, they found a sacerdotal caste all-powerful in most of the Scythic nations.

The original spirit of Zoroastrianism was fierce and exclusive. The early Iranians looked with contempt and hatred on the creed of their Indian brethren; they abhorred idolatry; and were disinclined to tolerate any religion except that which they had themselves worked out. But with the lapse of ages this spirit became softened. Polytheistic creeds are far less jealous than monotheism; and the development of Zoroastrianism had been in a polytheistic direction. By the time that the Zoroastrians were brought into contact with Magism, the first fervor of their religious zeal had abated, and they were in that intermediate condition of religious faith which at once impresses and is impressed, acts upon other systems, and allows itself to be acted upon in return. The result which supervened upon contact with Magism seems to have been a fusion, an absorption into Zoroastrianism of all the chief points of the Magian belief, and all the more remarkable of the Magian religious usages. This absorption appears to have taken place in Media. It was there that the Arian tribes first associated with themselves, and formally adopted into their body, the priest-caste of the Magi, which thenceforth was recognized as one of the six Median tribes. It is there that Magi are first found acting in the capacity of Arian priests. According to all the accounts which have come down to us, they soon acquired a predominating influence, which they no doubt used to impress their own religious doctrines more and more upon the nation at large, and to thrust into the background, so far as they dared, the peculiar features of the old Arian belief. It is not necessary to suppose that the Medes ever apostatized altogether from the worship of Ormazd, or formally surrendered their Dualistic faith. But, practically, the Magian doctrines and the Magian usages—elemental worship, divination with the sacred rods, dream expounding, incantations at the fire-altars, sacrifices whereat a Magus officiated—seem to have prevailed; the new predominated over the old; backed by the power of an organized hierarchy, Magism over-laid the primitive Arian creed, and, as time went on, tended more and more to become the real religion of the nation.

Among the religious customs introduced by the Magi into Media there are one or two which seem to require especial notice. The attribution of a sacred character to the four so-called elements—earth, air, fire and water—renders it extremely difficult to know what is to be done with the dead. They cannot be burnt, for that is a pollution of fire; or buried, for that is a pollution of earth; or thrown into a river, for that is a defilement of water. If they are deposited in sarcophagi, or exposed, they really pollute the air; but in this case the guilt of the pollution, it may be argued, does not rest on man, since the dead body is merely left in the element in which nature placed it. The only mode of disposal which completely avoids the defilement of every element is consumption of the dead by living beings; and the worship of the elements leads on naturally to this treatment of corpses. At present the Guebres, or Fire-worshippers, the descendants of the ancient Persians, expose all their dead, with the intention that they shall be devoured by birds of prey. In ancient times, it appears certain that the Magi adopted this practice with respect to their own dead; but, apparently, they did not insist upon having their example followed universally by the laity. Probably a natural instinct made the Arians averse to this coarse and revolting custom; and their spiritual guides, compassionating their weakness, or fearful of losing their own influence over them if they were too stiff in enforcing compliance, winked at the employment by the people of an entirely different practice. The dead bodies were first covered completely with a coating of wax, and were then deposited in the ground. It was held, probably, that the coating of wax prevented the pollution which would have necessarily resulted had the earth come into direct contact with the corpse.

The custom of divining by means of a number of rods appears to have been purely Magian. There is no trace of it in the Gathas, in the Yagna haptanhaiti, or in the older portions of the Vendidad. It was a Scythic practice; and probably the best extant account of it is that which Herodotus gives of the mode wherein it was managed by the Scyths of Europe. "Scythia," he says, "has an abundance of soothsayers, who foretell the future by means of a number of willow wands. A large bundle of these rods is brought and laid on the ground. The soothsayer unties the bundle, and places each wand by itself, at the same time uttering his prophecy: then, while he is still speaking, he gathers the rods together again, and makes them up once more into a bundle." A divine power seems to have been regarded as resting in the wands; and they were supposed to be "consulted" on the matter in hand, both severally and collectively. The bundle of wands thus imbued with supernatural wisdom became naturally part of the regular priestly costume, and was carried by the Magi on all occasions of ceremony. The wands were of different lengths; and the number of wands in the bundle varied. Sometimes there were three, sometimes five, sometimes as many as seven or nine; but in every case, as it would seem, an odd number.

Another implement which the priests commonly bore must be regarded, not as Magian, but as Zoroastrian. This is the khrafgthraghna, or instrument for killing bad animals, frogs, toads, snakes, mice, lizards, flies, etc., which belonged to the bad creation, or that which derived its origin from Angro-mainyus. These it was the general duty of all men, and the more especial duty of the Zoroastrian priests, to put to death, whenever they had the opportunity. The Magi, it appears, adopted this Arian usage, added the khrafgthraghna to the barsom, and were so zealous in their performance of the cruel work expected from them as to excite the attention, and even draw upon themselves the rebuke, of foreigners.

A practice is assigned to the Magi by many classical and ecclesiastical writers, which, if it were truly charged on them, would leave a very dark stain on the character of their ethical system. It is said that they allowed and even practised incest of the most horrible kind—such incest as we are accustomed to associate with the names of Lot, OEdipus, and Herod Agrippa. The charge seems to have been first made either by Xanthus the Lydian, or by Ctesias. It was accepted, probably without much inquiry, by the Greeks generally, and then by the Romans, was repeated by writer after writer as a certain fact, and became finally a stock topic with the early Christian apologists. Whether it had any real foundation in fact is very uncertain. Herodotus, who collects with so much pains the strange and unusual customs of the various nations whom he visits, is evidently quite ignorant of any such monstrous practice. He regards the Magian religion as established in Persia, yet he holds the incestuous marriage of Cambyses with his sister to have been contrary to existing Persian laws. At the still worst forms of incest of which the Magi and those under their influence are accused, Herodotus does not even glance. No doubt, if Xanthus Lydus really made the statement which Clemens of Alexandria assigns to him, it is an important piece of evidence, though scarcely sufficient to prove the Magi guilty. Xanthus was a man of little judgment, apt to relate extravagant tales; and, as a Lydian, he may have been disinclined to cast an aspersion on the religion of his country's oppressors. The passage in question, however, probably did not come from Xanthus Lydus, but from a much later writer who assumed his name, as has been well shown by a living critic. The true original author of the accusation against the Magi and their co-religionists seems to have been Ctesias, whose authority is far too weak to establish a charge intrinsically so improbable. Its only historical foundation seems to have been the fact that incestuous marriages were occasionally contracted by the Persian kings; not, however, in consequence of any law, or religious usage, but because in the plenitude of their power they could set all law at defiance, and trample upon the most sacred principles of morality and religion.

A minor charge preferred against the Magian morality by Xanthus, or rather by the pseudo-Xanthus, has possibly a more solid foundation. "The Magi," this writer said, "hold their wives in common: at least they often marry the wives of others with the free consent of their husbands." This is really to say that among the Magians divorce was over-facile; that wives were often put away, merely with a view to their forming a fresh marriage, by husbands who understood and approved of the transaction. Judging by the existing practice of the Persians, we must admit that such laxity is in accordance with Iranic notions on the subject of marriage—notions far less strict than those which have commonly prevailed among civilized nations. There is, however, no other evidence, besides this, that divorce was very common where the Magian system prevailed; and the mere assertion of the writer who personated Xanthus Lydus will scarcely justify us in affixing even this stigma on the religion.

Upon the whole, Magism, though less elevated and less pure than the old Zoroastrian creed, must be pronounced to have possessed a certain loftiness and picturesqueness which suited it to become the religion of a great and splendid monarchy. The mysterious fire-altars on the mountain-tops, with their prestige of a remote antiquity—the ever-burning flame believed to have been kindled from on high—the worship in the open air under the blue canopy of heaven—the long troops of Magians in their white robes, with their strange caps, and their mystic wands—the frequent prayers—the abundant sacrifices—the long incantations—the supposed prophetic powers of the priest-caste—all this together constituted an imposing whole at once to the eye and to the mind, and was calculated to give additional grandeur to the civil system that should be allied with it. Pure Zoroastrianism was too spiritual to coalesce readily with Oriental luxury and magnificence, or to lend strength to a government based on the ordinary principles of Asiatic despotism. Magism furnished a hierarchy to support the throne, and add splendor and dignity to the court, while they overawed the subject-class by their supposed possession of supernatural powers, and of the right of mediating between heaven and man. It supplied a picturesque worship which at once gratified the senses and excited the fancy It gave scope to man's passion for the marvellous by its incantations, its divining-rods, its omen-reading, and its dream-expounding. It gratified the religious scrupulosity which finds a pleasure in making to itself difficulties, by the disallowance of a thousand natural acts, and the imposition of numberless rules for external purity. At the same time it gave no offence to the anti-idolatrous spirit in which the Arians had hitherto gloried, but rather encouraged the iconoclasm which they always upheld and practised. It thus blended easily with the previous creed of the people, awaking no prejudices, clashing with no interests; winning its way by an apparent meekness and unpresumingness, while it was quite prepared, when the fitting time came, to be as fierce and exclusive as if it had never worn the mask of humility and moderation.

CHAPTER V

LANGUAGE AND WRITING

On the language of the ancient Medes a very few observations will be here made. It has been noticed already that the Median form of speech was closely allied to that of the Persians. The remark of Strabo quoted above, and another remark which he cites from Nearchus, imply at once this fact, and also the further fact of a dialectic difference between the two tongues. Did we possess, as some imagine that we do, materials for tracing out this diversity, it would be proper in the present place to enter fully on the subject, and instead of contenting ourselves with asserting, or even proving, the substantial oneness of the languages, it would be our duty to proceed to the far more difficult and more complicated task of comparing together the sister dialects, and noting their various differences. The supposition that there exist means for such a comparison is based upon a theory that in the language of the Zendavesta we have the true speech of the ancient people of Media, while in the cuneiform inscriptions of the Achæmenian kings it is beyond controversy that we possess the ancient language of Persia. It becomes necessary, therefore, to examine this theory, in order to justify our abstention from an inquiry on which, if the theory were sound, we should be now called upon to enter.

The notion that the Zend language was the idiom of ancient Media originated with Anquetil du Perron. He looked on Zoroaster as a native of Azerbijan, contemporary with Darius Hystaspis. His opinion was embraced by Kleuker, Herder, and Eask; and again, with certain modifications, by Tychsen and Heeren. These latter writers even gave a more completely Median character to the Zendavesta, by regarding it as composed in Media Magna, during the reign of the great Cyaxares. The main foundation of these views was the identification of Zoroastrianism with the Magian fire-worship, which was really ancient in Azerbijan, and flourished in Media under the great Median monarch. But we have seen that Magianism and Zoroastrianism were originally entirely distinct, and that the Zendavesta in all its earlier portions belongs wholly to the latter system. Nothing therefore is proved concerning the Zend dialect by establishing a connection between the Medes and Magism, which was a corrupting influence thrown in upon Zoroastrianism long after the composition of the great bulk of the sacred writings.

These writings themselves sufficiently indicate the place of their composition. It was not Media, but Bactria, or at any rate the north-eastern Iranic country, between the Bolor range and the Caspian. This conclusion, which follows from a consideration of the various geographical notices contained in the Zend books, had been accepted of late years by all the more profound Zend scholars. Originated by Rhode, it has also in its favor the names of Burnouf, Lassen, Westergaard, and Haug. If then the Zend is to be regarded as really a local dialect, the idiom of a particular branch of the Iranic people, there is far more reason for considering it to be the ancient speech of Bactria than of any other Arian country. Possibly the view is correct which recognizes two nearly-allied dialects as existing side by side in Iran during its flourishing period—one prevailing towards the west, the other towards the east—one Medo-Persic, the other Sogdo-Bactrian—the former represented to us by the cuneiform inscriptions, the latter by the Zend texts. Or it may be closer to the truth to recognize in the Zendic and Achæmenian forms of speech, not so much two contemporary idioms, as two stages of one and the same language, which seems to be at present the opinion of the best comparative philologists. In either case Media can claim no special interest in Zend, which, if local, is Sogdo-Bactrian, and if not local is no more closely connected with Media than with Persia.

It appears then that we do not at present possess any means of distinguishing the shades of difference which separated the. Median from the Persian speech. We have in fact no specimens of the former beyond a certain number of words, and those chiefly proper names, whereas we know the latter tolerably completely from the inscriptions. It is proposed under the head of the "Fifth Monarchy" to consider at some length the general character of the Persian language as exhibited to us in these documents. From the discussion then to be raised may be gathered the general character of the speech of the Medes. In the present place all that will be attempted is to show how far the remnants left us of Median speech bear out the statement that, substantially, one and the same tongue was spoken by both peoples.

Many Median names are absolutely identical with Persian; e.g., Ariobarzanes, Artabazus, Artaeus, Artembares, Harpagus, Arbaces, Tiridates, etc. Others which are not absolutely identical approach to the Persian form so closely as to be plainly mere variants, like Theodoras and Theodosius, Adelbert and Ethelbert, Miriam, Mariam, and Mariamne. Of this kind are Intaphres, another form of Intaphernes, Artynes, another form of Artanes, Parmises, another form of Parmys, and the like. A third class, neither identical with any known Persian names, nor so nearly approaching to them as to be properly considered mere variants, are made up of known Persian roots, and may be explained on exactly the same principles as Persian names. Such are Ophernes, Sitraphernes, Mitraphernes, Megabernes, Aspadas, Mazares, Tachmaspates, Xathrites, Spitaces, Spitamas, Ehambacas, and others. In Ophernes, Sitra-phernes, Mitra-phernes, and Mega-bernes, the second element is manifestly the pharna or frana which is found in Arta-phernes and Inta-phernes (Vida-frana), an active participial form from pri, to protect. The initial element in O-phernes represents the Zend hu, Sans, su, Greek ev, as the same letter does in O-manes, O-martes, etc. The Sitra of Sitra-phernes has been explained as probably Ichshatra, "the crown," which is similarly represented in the Safro-pates of Curtius, a name standing to Sitra-phernes exactly as Arta-patas to Arta-phernes. In Mega-bernes the first element is the well-known baga, "God," under the form commonly preferred by the Greeks; and the name is exactly equivalent to Curtius's Bagfo-phanes, which only differs from it by taking the participle of pa, "to protect," instead of the participle of pri, which has the same meaning. In Aspa-das it is easy to recognize aspa, "horse" (a common root in Persian names,) e.g., Aspa-thines, Aspa-mitras, Prex-aspes, and the like, followed by the same element which terminates the name of Oromaz-des, and which means either "knowing" or "giving." Ma-zares presents us with the root meh, "much" or "great," which is found in the name of the ilf-aspii, or "Big Horses," a Persian tribe, followed by zara, "gold," which appears in Ctesias's "Arto-awes," and perhaps also in Zoro-aster. In Tachmaspates, the first element is takhma, "strong," a root found in the Persian names Ar-tochmes and Tritan-taechmes, while the second is the frequently used pati, "lord," which occurs as the initial element in Pak-zeithes," Pafa-ramphes, etc., and as the terminal in Pharna-jjates, Avio-peithes, and the like. In Xathrites we have clearly khshatra (Zend khshathra), "crown" or "king," with a participial suffix -ita, corresponding to the Sanscrit termination in -it. Spita-ces and Spita-mas contain the root spita, equivalent to spenta, "holy," which is found in Spitho-hates, Spita-mens, Spita-des, etc. This, in Spita-ces, is followed by a guttural ending, which is either a diminutive corresponding to the modern Persian -efc, or perhaps a suffixed article. In Spit-amas, the suffix -mas is the common form of the superlative, and may be compared with the Latin -mus in optimus, intimus, supremus, and the like. Ehambacas contains the root rafno, "joy, pleasure," which we find in Pati-ramphies, followed by the guttural suffix.

There remains, finally, a class of Median names, containing roots not found in any known names of Persians, but easily explicable from Zend, Sanscrit, or other cognate tongues, and therefore not antagonistic to the view that Median and Persian were two closely connected dialects. Such, for instance, are the royal names mentioned by Herodotus, Deioces, Phraortes, Astyages, and Cyaxares; and such also are the following, which come to us from various sources; Amytis, Astibaras, Armamithres or Harmamithres, Mandauces, Parsondas, Eama-tes, Susiscanes, Tithaous, and Zanasanes.

In Deioces, or (as the Latins write it) Dejoces, there can be little doubt that we have the name given as Djohak or Zohak in the Shahnameh and other modern Persian writings, which is itself an abbreviation of the Ajis-dahaka of the Zendavesta. Dahaka means in Zend "biting," or "the biter," and is etymo-logically connected with the Greek.

Phraortes, which in old Persian was Fravartish, seems to be a mere variant of the word which appears in the Zendavesta as fravashi, and designates each man's tutelary genius. The derivation is certainly from fra, and probably from a root akin to the German wahren, French garder, English "ward, watch," etc. The meaning is "a protector."

Cyaxares, the Persian form of which was "Uvakhshatara," seems to be formed from the two elements it or hu, "well, good," and akhsha (Zend arsnd), "the eye," which is the final element of the name Cyavarswa in the Zendavesta. Cyavarsna is "dark-eyed;" Uvakhsha (= Zend Huvarsna) would be "beautiful-eyed." Uvakhshatara appears to be the comparative of this adjective, and would mean "more beautiful-eyed (than others)."

Astyages, which, according to Moses of Chorene, meant "a dragon" or "serpent," is almost certainly Ajis-dahaka, the full name whereof Dojoces (or Zohak) is the abbreviation. It means "the biting snake," from aji or azi, "a snake" or "serpent," and dahaka, "biting."

Amytis is probably ama, "active, great," with the ordinary feminine suffix -iti, found in Armaiti, Khnathaiti, and the like. Astibaras is perhaps "great of bone," from Zend agta (Sans, asthi), "bone," and bereza, "tall, great." Harmamithres, if that is the true reading, would be "mountain-lover" (monticolus), from hardam, ace. of hara, "a mountain," and mithra or mitra, "fond of." If, however, the name should be read as Armamithres, the probable derivation will be from rama, ace. of raman, "pleasure," which is also the root of Rama-tea. Armamithres may then be compared with Rheomithres, Siromitras, and Sysimithres, which are respectively "fond of splendor," "fond of beauty," and "fond of light." Mandauces is perhaps "biting spirit—esprit mordant," from mand, "coeur, esprit," and dahaka, "biting." M Parsondas can scarcely be the original form, from the occurrence in it of the nasal before the dental. In the original it must have been Parsodas, which would mean "liberal, much giving," from pourus, "much," and da, "to give." Ramates, as already observed, is from rama, "pleasure." It is an adjectival form, like Datis, and means probably "pleasant, agreeable." Susiscanes may be explained as "splendidus juvenis," from quc, "splendere," pres. part, cao-cat, and kainin, "adolescens, juvenis." Tithaeus is probably for Tathaeus, which would be readily formed from tatka, "one who makes." Finally, Zanasanes may be referred to the root zan or jan, "to kill," which is perhaps simply followed by the common appellative suffix -ana.

From these names of persons we may pass to those of places in Media, which equally admit of explanation from roots known to have existed either in Zend or in old Persian. Of these, Ecbatana, Bagistana, and Aspadana may be taken as convenient specimens. Ecbatana (or Agbatana), according to the orthography of the older Greeks was in the native dialect Hagmatana, as appears from the Behistun inscription. This form, Hagmatana, is in all probability derived from the three words ham, "with" (Sans, sam, Latin cum), gam, "to go" (Zend gd, Sans, 'gam), and ctana (Mod. Pers. -stan) "a place." The initial ham has dropped the m and become ha, and cum becomes co- in Latin; gam has become gma by metathesis; and gtan has passed into -tan by phonetic corruption. Ha-gma-tana would be "the place for assembly," or for "coming together" (Lat. comitium); the place, i.e., where the tribes met, and where, consequently, the capital grew up.

Bagistan, which was "a hill sacred to Jupiter" according to Diodorus, is clearly a name corresponding to the Beth-el of the Hebrews and the Allahabad of the Mahometans. It is simply "the house, or place, of God"—from baga, "God," and gtana, "place, abode," the common modern Persian terminal (compare Farsi-stan, Khuzi-stan, Afghani-stan, Belochi-stan, Hindu-stan, etc.), which has here not suffered any corruption.

Aspadana contains certainly as its first element the root acpa, "horse." The suffix dan may perhaps be a corruption of ctana, analogous to that which has produced Hama-dan from Hagma-ctan; or it may be a contracted form of danhu, or dairihu, "a-province," Aspadana having been originally the name of a district where horses were bred, and having thence become the name of its chief town.

The Median words known to us, other than names of persons or places, are confined to some three or four. Herodotus tells us that the Median word for "dog" was spaka; Xenophon implies, if he does not expressly state, that the native name for the famous Median robe was candys; Nicolas of Damascus informs us that the Median couriers were called Angari; and Hesychius says that the artabe was a Median measure. The last-named writer also states that artades and devas were Magian words, which perhaps implies that they were common to the Medes with the Persians. Here, again, the evidence, such as it is, favors a close connection between the languages of Media and Persia.

That artabe and angarus were Persian words no less than Median, we have the evidence of Herodotus. Artades, "just men" (according to Hesychhis), is probably akin to ars, "true, just," and may represent the ars-data, "made just," of the Zendavesta. Devas (Seven), which Hesychius translates "the evil gods" is clearly the Zendic daiva, Mod. Pers. div. (Sans, deva, Lat. divus). In candys we have most probably a formation from qan, "to dress, to adorn." Spaka is the Zendic cpa, with the Scythic guttural suffix, of which the Medes were so fond, cpa itself being akin to the Sanscrit cvan, and so to hvoov and canis. Thus we may connect all the few words which are known as Median with forms contained in the Zend, which was either the mother or the elder sister of the ancient Persian.

That the Medes were acquainted with the art of writing, and practised it—at least from the time that they succeeded to the dominion of the Assyrians—scarcely admits of a doubt. An illiterate nation, which conquers one in possession of a literature, however it may despise learning and look down upon the mere literary life, is almost sure to adopt writing to some extent on account of its practical utility. It is true the Medes have left us no written monuments; and we may fairly conclude from that fact that they used writing sparingly; but besides the antecedent probability, there is respectable evidence that letters were known to them, and that, at any rate, their upper classes could both read and write their native tongue. The story of the letter sent by Harpagus the Mede to Cyrus in the belly of a hare, though probably apocryphal, is important as showing the belief of Herodotus on the subject. The still more doubtful story of a despatch written on parchment by a Median king, Artseus, and sent to Nanarus, a provincial governor, related by Nicolas of Damascus, has a value, as indicating that writer's conviction that the Median monarchs habitually conveyed their commands to their subordinates in a written form. With these statements of profane writers agree certain notices which we find in Scripture. Darius the Mode, shortly after the destruction of the Median empire, "signs" a decree, which his chief nobles have presented to him in writing. He also himself "writes" another decree addressed to his subjects generally. In later times we find that there existed at the Persian court a "book of the chronicles of the kings of Media and Persia," in which was probably a work begun under the Median and continued under the Persian sovereigns.

If then writing was practised by the Medes, it becomes interesting to consider whence they obtained their knowledge of it, and what was the system which they employed. Did they bring an alphabet with them from the far East, or did they derive their first knowledge of letters from the nations with whom they came into contact after their great migration? In the latter case, did they adopt, with or without modifications, a foreign system, or did they merely borrow the idea of written symbols from their new neighbors, and set to work to invent for themselves an alphabet suited to the genius of their own tongue? These are some of the questions which present themselves to the mind as deserving of attention, when this subject is brought before it. Unfortunately we possess but very scanty data for determining, and can do little more than conjecture, the proper answers to be given to them.

The early composition of certain portions of the Zendavesta, which has been asserted in this work, may seem at first sight to imply the use of a written character in Bactria and the adjacent countries at a very remote era. But such a conclusion is not necessary. Nations have often had an oral literature, existing only in the memories of men, and have handed down such a literature from generation to generation, through a long succession of ages. The sacred lore of Zoroaster may have been brought by the Modes from the East-Caspian country in an unwritten shape, and may not have been reduced to writing till many centuries later. On the whole it is perhaps most probable that the Medes were unacquainted with letters when they made their great migration, and that they acquired their first knowledge of them from the races with whom they came into collision when they settled along the Zagros chain. In these regions they were brought into contact with at least two forms of written speech, one that of the old Armenians, a Turanian dialect, the other that of the Assyrians, a language of the Semitic type. These two nations used the same alphabetic system, though their languages were utterly unlike; and it would apparently have been the easiest plan for the new comers to have adopted the established forms, and to have applied them, so far as was possible, to the representation of their own speech. But the extreme complication of a system which employed between three and four hundred written signs, and composed signs sometimes of fourteen or fifteen wedges, seems to have shocked the simplicity of the Medes, who recognized the fact that the varieties of their articulations fell far short of this excessive luxuriance. The Arian races, so far as appears, declined to follow the example set them by the Turanians of Armenia, who had adopted the Assyrian alphabet, and preferred to invent a new system for themselves, which they determined to make far more simple. It is possible that they found an example already set them. In Achaemenian times we observe two alphabets used through Media and Persia, both of which are simpler than the Assyrian: one is employed to express the Turanian dialect of the people whom the Arians conquered and dispossessed; the other, to express the tongue of the conquerors. It is possible—though we have no direct evidence of the fact—that the Turanians of Zagros and the neighborhood had already formed for themselves the alphabet which is found in the second columns of the Achaemenian tablets, when the Arian invaders conquered them. This alphabet, which in respect of complexity holds an intermediate position between the luxuriance of the Assyrian and the simplicity of the Medo-Persic system, would seem in all probability to have intervened in order of time between the two. It consists of no more than about a hundred characters, and these are for the most part far less complicated than those of Assyria. If the Medes found this form of writing already existing in Zagros when they arrived, it may have assisted to give them the idea of making for themselves an alphabet so far on the old model that the wedge should be the sole element used in the formation, of letters, but otherwise wholly new, and much more simple than those previously in use.

Discarding then the Assyrian notion of a syllabarium, with the enormous complication which it involves, the Medes strove to reduce sounds to their ultimate elements, and to represent these last alone by symbols. Contenting themselves with the three main vowel sounds, a,i, and u, and with one breathing, a simple h, they recognized twenty consonants, which were the following, b,d,f,g,j,k,kh,m,n,n (sound doubtful), p,r,s,sh,t,v,y,z,ch (as in much), and tr, an unnecessary compound. Had they stopped here, their characters should have been but twenty-four, the number which is found in Greek. To their ears, however, it would seem, each consonant appeared to carry with it a short a, and as this, occurring before i and u, produced the diphthongs ai and au, sounded nearly as e and o, it seemed necessary, where a consonant was to be directly followed by the sounds i or u, to have special forms to which the sound of a should not attach. This system, carried out completely, would have raised the forms of consonants to sixty, a multiplication that was feared as inconvenient. In order to keep down the number, it seems to have been resolved, that one form should suffice for the aspirated letters and the sibilants (viz., h,kh; ch,ph or f,s,sh, and z), and also for b,y, and tr; that two forms should suffice for the tenues, k,p,t, for the liquids n and r, and for v; and consequently that the full number of three forms should be limited to some three or four letters, as d, m, j, and perhaps g. The result is that the known alphabet of the Persians, which is assumed here to have been the invention of the Medes, consists of some thirty-six or thirty-seven forms, which are really representative of no more than twenty-three distinct sounds.

It appears then that, compared with the phonetic systems in vogue among their neighbors, the alphabet of the Medes and Persians was marked by a great simplicity. The forms of the letters were also very much simplified. Instead of conglomerations of fifteen or sixteen wedges in a single character, we have in the Medo-Persic letters a maximum of five wedges. The most ordinary number is four, which is sometimes reduced to three or even two. The direction of the wedges is uniformly either perpendicular or horizontal, except of course in the case of the double wedge or arrow-head, where the component elements are placed obliquely. The arrow-head has but one position, the perpendicular, with the angle facing towards the left hand. The only diagonal sign used is a simple wedge, placed obliquely with the point towards the right, which is a mere mark of separation between the words.

The direction of the writing was, as with the Arian nations generally, from left to right. Words were frequently divided, and part carried on to the next line. The characters were inscribed between straight lines drawn from end to end of the tablet on which they were written. Like the Hebrew, they often closely resembled one another, and a slight defect in the stone will cause one to be mistaken for another. The resemblance is not between letters of the same class or kind; on the contrary, it is often between those which are most remote from one another. Thus g nearly resembles u; ch is like d; tr like p; and so on: while k and kh, s and sh, p and ph (or J) are forms quite dissimilar.

It is supposed that a cuneiform alphabet can never have been employed for ordinary writing purposes, but must have been confined to documents of some importance, which it was desirable to preserve, and which were therefore either inscribed on stone, or impressed on moist clay afterwards baked. A cursive character, it is therefore imagined, must always have been in use, parallel with a cuneiform one; and as the Babylonians and Assyrians are known to have used a character of this kind from a very high antiquity, synchronously with their lapidary cuneiform, so it is supposed that the Arian races must have possessed, besides the method which has been described as a cursive system of writing. Of this, however, there is at present no direct evidence. No cursive writing of the Arian nations at this time, either Median or Persian, has been found; and it is therefore uncertain what form of character they employed on common occasions.

The material used for ordinary purposes, according to Nicolas of Damascus and Ctesias, was parchment. On this the kings wrote the despatches which conveyed their orders to the officers who administered the government of provinces; and on this were inscribed the memorials which each monarch was careful to have composed giving an account of the chief events of his reign. The cost of land carriage probably prevented papyrus from superseding this material in Western Asia, as it did in Greece at a tolerably early date. Clay, so much used for writing on both in Babylonia and Assyria, appears never to have approved itself as a convenient substance to the Iranians. For public documents the chisel and the rock, for private the pen and the prepared skin, seem to have been preferred by them; and in the earlier times, at any rate, they employed no other materials.

CHAPTER VI

CHRONOLOGY AND HISTORY

Media . . . quam ante regnum Cyri superlovis et incrementa Persidos legimus Asiae reginam totius.— Amm. Marc, xxiii. 6.

The origin of the Median nation is wrapt in a profound obscurity. Following the traces which the Zendavesta offers, taking into consideration its minute account of the earlier Arian migrations, its entire omission of any mention of the Medes, and the undoubted fact that it was nevertheless by the Medes and Persians that the document itself was preserved and transmitted to us, we should be naturally led to suppose that the race was one which in the earlier times of Arian development was weak and insignificant, and that it first pushed itself into notice after the ethnological portions of the Zendavesta were composed, which is thought to have been about B.C. 1000. Quite in accordance with this view is the further fact that in the native Assyrian annals, so far as they have been, recovered, the Medes do not make their appearance till the middle of the ninth century B.C., and when they appear are weak and unimportant, only capable of opposing a very slight resistance to the attacks of the Ninevite kings. The natural conclusion from these data would appear to be that until about B.C. 850 the Median name was unknown in the world, and that previously, if Medes existed at all, it was either as a sub-tribe of some other Arian race, or at any rate as a tribe too petty and insignificant to obtain mention either on the part of native or of foreign historians. Such early insignificance and late development of what ultimately becomes the dominant tribe of a race is no strange or unprecedented phenomenon to the historical inquirer; on the contrary, it is among the facts with which he is most familiar, and would admit of ample illustration, were the point worth pursuing, alike from the history of the ancient and the modern world.

But, against the conclusion to which we could not fail to be led by the Arian and Assyrian records, which agree together so remarkably, two startling notices in works of great authority but of a widely different character have to be set. In the Toldoth Beni Noah, or "Book of the Generation of the Sons of Noah," which forms the tenth chapter of Genesis, and which, if the work of Moses, was probably composed at least as early as B.C. 1500, we find the Madai—a word elsewhere always signifying "the Medes"—in the genealogy of the sons of Japhet. The word is there conjoined with several other important ethnic titles, as Gomer, Magog, Javan, Tubal, and Meshech; and there can be no reasonable doubt that it is intended to designate the Median people. If so, the people must have had already a separate and independent existence in the fifteenth century B.C., and not only so, but they must have by that time attained so much distinction as to be thought worthy of mention by a writer who was only bent on affiliating the more important of the nations known to him.

The other notice is furnished by Berosus. That remarkable historian, in his account of the early dynasties of his native Chaldaea, declared that, at a date anterior to B.C. 2000, the Medes had conquered Babylon by a sudden inroad, had established a monarchy there, and had held possession of the city and neighboring territory for a period of 224 years. Eight kings of their race had during that interval occupied the Babylonian throne, It has been already observed that this narrative must represent a fact. Berosus would not have gratuitously invented a foreign conquest of his native land; nor would the earlier Babylonians, from whom he derived his materials, have forged a tale which was so little flattering to their national vanity. Some foreign conquest of Babylon must have taken place about the period named; and it is certainly a most important fact that Berosus should call the conquerors Medes. He may no doubt have been mistaken about an event so ancient; he may have misread his authorities, or he may have described as Medes a people of which he really knew nothing except that they had issued from the tract which in his own time bore the name of Media. But, while these axe mere possibilities, hypotheses to which the mind resorts in order to escape a difficulty, the hard fact remains that he has used the word; and this fact, coupled with the mention of the Medes in the book of Genesis, does certainly raise a presumption of no inconsiderable strength against, the view which it would be natural to take if the Zendavesta and the Assyrian annals were our solo authorities on the subject. It lends a substantial basis to the theories of those who regard the Medes as one of the principal primeval races; who believe that they were well known to the Semitic inhabitants of the Mesopotamian valley as early as the twenty-third century before Christ—long ere Abraham left Ur for Harran; and that they actually formed the dominant power in Western Asia for more than two centuries, prior to the establishment of the first Chaldaean kingdom.

And if there are thus distinct historical grounds for the notion of an early Median development, there are not wanting these obscurer but to many minds more satisfactory proofs wherewith comparative philology and ethnology are wont to illustrate and confirm the darker passages of ancient history. Recent linguistic research has clearly traced among the Arba Lisun, or, "Four Tongues" of ancient Chaldaea, which are so often mentioned on the ancient monuments, an Arian formation, such as would naturally have been left in the country, if it had been occupied for some considerable period by a dominant Arian power. The early Chaldaean ideographs have often several distinct values; and when this is the case, one of the powers is almost always an Arian name of the object represented. Words like nir, "man", ar, "river," (compare the names Aras, Araxes, Endanus, Rha, Rhodanus, etc., the Slavonic rika, "river," etc.), san, "sun," (compare German Sonne, Slavonic solnce, English "sun," Dutch zon, etc.), are seemingly Arian roots; and the very term "Arian" (Ariya, "noble") is perhaps contained in the name of a primitive Chaldaean monarch, "Arioch, king of Ellasar." There is nothing perhaps in these scattered traces of Arian influence in in Lower Mesopotamia at a remote era that points very particularly to the Medes; but at any rate they harmonize with the historical account that has reached us of early Arian power in these parts, and it is important that they should not be ignored when we are engaged in considering the degree of credence that is to be awarded to the account in question.

Again, there are traces of a vast expansion, apparently at a very early date, of the Median race, such as seems to imply that they must have been a great nation in Western Asia long previously to the time of the Iranic movements in Bactria and the adjoining regions. In the Matieni of Zagros and Cappadocia, in the Sauro-matae (or Northern Medes) of the country between the Palus Maeotis and the Caspian, in the Maetae or Maeotae of the tract about the mouth of the Don, and in the Maedi of Thrace, we have seemingly remnants of a great migratory host which, starting from the mountains that overhang Mesopotamia, spread itself into the regions of the north and the north-west at a time which does not admit of being definitely stated, but which is clearly anti-historic. Whether these races generally retained any tradition of their origin, we do not know; but a tribe which in the time of Herodotus dwelt still further to the west than even the Maedi—to wit, the Sigynnae, who occupied the tract between the Adriatic and the Danube—had a very distinct belief in their Median descent, a belief confirmed by the resemblance which their national dress bore to that of the Medes. Herodotus, who relates these facts concerning them, appends an expression of his astonishment at the circumstance that emigrants from Media should have proceeded to such a distance from their original home; how it had been brought about he could not conceive. "Still," he sagaciously remarks, "nothing is impossible in the long lapse of ages."

A further argument in favor of the early development of Median power, and the great importance of the nation in Western Asia at a period anterior to the ninth century, is derivable from the ancient legends of the Greeks, which seem to have designated the Medes under the two eponyms of Medea and Andromeda. These legends indeed do not admit of being dated with any accuracy; but as they are of a primitive type, and probably older than Homer, we cannot well assign them to an age later than b.c. 1000. Now they connect the Median name with the two countries of Syria and Colchis, countries remote from each other, and neither of them sufficiently near the true Median territory to be held from it, unless at a time when the Medes were in possession of something like an empire. And, even apart from any inferences to be drawn from the localties which the Greek Myths connect with the Medes, the very fact that the race was known to the Greeks at this early date—long before the movements which brought them into contact with the Assyrians—would seem to show that there was some remote period—prior to the Assyrian domination—when the fame of the Medes was great in the part of Asia known to the Hellenes, and that they did not first attract Hellenic notice (as, but for the Myths, we might have imagined) by the conquests of Cyaxarea. Thus, on the whole it would appear that we must acknowledge two periods of Median prosperity, separated from each other by a lengthy interval, one anterior to the rise of the Cushite empire in Lower Babylonia, the other parallel with the decline and subsequently to the fall of Assyria.

Of the first period it cannot be said that we possess any distinct historical knowledge. The Median dynasty of Berosus at Babylon appears, by recent discoveries, to have represented those Susianian monarchs who bore sway there from B.C. 2286 to 2052. The early Median preponderance in Western

Asia, if it is a fact, must have been anterior to this, and is an event which has only left traces in ethnological names and in mythological speculations.

Our historical knowledge of the Medes as a nation commences in the latter half of the ninth century before our era. Shalmaneser II.—probably the "Shalman" of Hosea,—who reigned from B.C. 859 to B.C. 824—relates that in his twenty-fourth year (B.C. 885), after having reduced to subjection the Zimri, who held the Zagros mountain range immediately to the east of Assyria, and received tribute from the Persians, he led an expedition into Media and Arazias, where he took and destroyed a number of the towns, slaying the men, and carrying off the spoil. He does not mention any pitched battle; and indeed it would seem that he met with no serious resistance. The Medes whom he attacks are evidently a weak and insignificant people, whom he holds in small esteem, and regards as only deserving of a hurried mention. They seem to occupy the tract now known as Ardelan—a varied region containing several lofty ridges, with broad plains lying between them.

It is remarkable that the time of this first contact of Media with Assyria—a contact taking place when Assyria was in her prime, and Media was only just emerging from a long period of weakness and obscurity—is almost exactly that which Ctesias selects as a day of the great revolution whereby the Empire of the East passed from the hands of the Shemites into those of the Arians. The long residence of Otesias among the Persians, gave him a bias toward that people, which even extended to their close kin, the Medes. Bent on glorifying these two Arian races, he determined to throw back the commencement of their empire to a period long anterior to the true date; and, feeling specially anxious to cover up their early humiliation, he assigned their most glorious conquests to the very century, and almost to the very time, when they were in fact suffering reverses at the hands of the people over whom he represented them as triumphant. There was a boldness in the notion of thus inverting history which almost deserved, and to a considerable extent obtained, success. The "long chronology" of Ctesias kept its ground until recently, not indeed meeting with universal acceptance, but on the whole predominating over the "short chronology" of Herodotus; and it may be doubted whether anything less than the discovery that the native records of Assyria entirely contradicted Ctesias would have sufficed to drive from the field his figment of early Median dominion.

The second occasion upon which we hear of the Medes in the Assyrian annals is in the reign of Shalmanoser's son and successor, Shamas-Vul. Here again, as on the former occasion, the Assyrians were the aggressors. Shamas-Vul invaded Media and Arazias in his third year, and committed ravages similar to those of his father, wasting the country with fire and sword, but not (it would seem) reducing the Medes to subjection, or even attempting to occupy their territory. Again the attack is a mere raid, which produces no permanent impression.

It is in the reign of the son and successor of Shamas-Vul that the Medes appear for the first time to have made their submission and accepted the position of Assyrian tributaries. A people which was unable to offer effectual resistance when the Assyrian levies invaded their country, and which had no means of retaliating upon their foe or making him suffer the evils that he inflicted, was naturally tempted to save itself from molestation by the payment of an annual tribute, so purchasing quiet at the expense of honor and independence. Towards the close of the ninth century B.C. the Medes seem to have followed the example set them very much earlier by their kindred and neighbors, the Persians, and to have made arrangements for an annual payment which should exempt their territory from ravage. It is doubtful whether the arrangement was made by the whole people. The Median tribes at this time hung so loosely together that a policy adopted by one portion of them might be entirely repudiated by another. Most probably the tribute was paid by those tribes only which boarded on Zagros, and not by those further to the east or to the north, into whose territories the Assyrian arms has not yet penetrated.

No further change in the condition of the Medes is known to have occurred until about a hundred years later, when the Assyrians ceased to be content with the semi-independent position which had been hitherto allowed them, and determined on their more complete subjugation. The great Sargon, the assailant of Egypt and conqueror of Babylon, towards the middle of his reign, invaded Media with a large army, and having rapidly overrun the country, seized several of the towns, and "annexed them to Assyria," while at the same time he also established in new situations a number of fortified posts. The object was evidently to incorporate Media into the empire; and the posts wore stations in which a standing army was placed, to overawe the natives and prevent them from offering an effectual resistance. With the same view deportation of the people on a large scale seems to have been practised and the gaps thus made in the population were filled up—wholly or in part—by the settlement in the Median cities of Samaritan captives. On the country thus re-organized and re-arranged a tribute of a new character was laid. In lieu of the money payment hitherto exacted, the Medes were required to furnish annually to the royal stud a number of horses. It is probable that Media was already famous for the remarkable breed which is so celebrated in later times; and that the horses now required of her by the Assyrians were to be of the large and highly valued kind known as "Nisaean."

The date of this subjugation is about B.C. 710. And here, if we compare the Greek accounts of Median history with those far more authentic ones which have reached us through the Assyrian contemporary records, we are struck by a repetition of the same device which came under our notice more than a century earlier—the device of covering up the nation's disgraces at a particular period by assigning to that very date certain great and striking successes. As Ctesias's revolt of the Medes under Arbaces and conquest of Nineveh synchronizes nearly with the first known ravages of Assyria within the territories of the Medes, so Herodotus's revolt of the same people and commencement of their monarchy under Deioces falls almost exactly at the date when they entirely lose their independence. As there is no reason to suspect Herodotus either of partiality toward the Medes or of any wilful departure from the truth, we must regard him as imposed upon by his informants, who were probably either Medes or Persians. These mendacious patriots found little difficulty in palming their false tale upon the simple Halicarnassian, thereby at once extending the antiquity of their empire and concealing its shame behind a halo of fictitious glory.

After their subjugation by Sargon the Medes of Media Magna appear to have remained the faithful subjects of Assyria for sixty or seventy years. During this period we find no notices of the great mass of the nation in the Assyrian records: only here and there indications occur that Assyria is stretching out her arms towards the more distant and outlying tribes, especially those of Azerbijan, and compelling them to acknowledge her as mistress. Sennacherib boasts that early in his reign, about B.C. 702, he received an embassy from the remoter parts of Media—"parts of which the kings his fathers had not even heard"—which brought him presents in sign of submission, and patiently accepted his yoke. His son, Esar-haddon, relates that, about his tenth year (B.C. 671) he invaded Bikni or Bikan, a distant province of Media, "whereof the kings his fathers had never heard the name;" and, attacking the cities of the region one after another, forced them to acknowledge his authority. The country was held by a number of independent chiefs, each bearing sway in his own city and adjacent territory. These chiefs have unmistakably Arian names, as Sitriparna or Sitraphernes, Eparna or Orphernes, Zanasana or Zanasanes, and Eamatiya or Ramates. Esar-haddon says that, having entered the country with his army, he seized two of the chiefs and carried them off to Assyria, together with a vast spoil and numerous other captives. Hereupon the remaining chiefs, alarmed for their safety, made their submission, consenting to pay an annual tribute, and admitting Assyrian officers into their territories, who watched, if they did not even control, the government.

We are now approaching the time when Media seems to have been first consolidated into a monarchy by the genius of an individual. Sober history is forced to discard the shadowy forms of kings with which Greek writers of more fancy than judgment have peopled the darkness that rests upon the "origines" of the Medes. Arbaces, Maudaces, Sosarmus, Artycas, Arbianes, Artseus, Deioces—Median monarchs, according to Ctesias or Herodotus, during the space of time comprised within the years B.C. 875 and 655—have to be dismissed by the modern writer without a word, since there is reason to believe that they are mere creatures of the imagination, inventions of unscrupulous romancers, not men who once walked the earth. The list of Median kings in Ctesias, so far as it differs from the list in Herodotus, seems to be a pure forgery—an extension of the period of the monarchy by the conscious use of a system of duplication. Each king, or period, in Herodotus occurs in the list of Ctesias twice—a transparent device, clumsily cloaked by the cheap expedient of a liberal invention of names. Even the list of Herodotus requires curtailment. His Deioces, whose whole history reads more like romance than truth—the organizer of a powerful monarchy in Media just at the time when Sargon was building his fortified posts in the country and peopling with his Israelite captives the old "cities of the Medes"—the prince who reigned for above half a century in perfect peace with his neighbors, and who, although contemporary with Sargon, Sennacherib, Esar-haddon, and As-shur-bani-pal—all kings more or less connected with Media—is never heard of in any of their annals, must be relegated to the historical limbo in which repose so many "shades of mighty names;" and the Herodotean list of Median kings must at any rate, be thus far reduced. Nothing is more evident than that during the flourishing period of Assyria under the great Sargonidae above named there was no grand Median kingdom upon the eastern flank of the empire. Such a kingdom had certainly not been formed up to B.C. 671, when Esar-haddon reduced the more distant Medes, finding them still under the government of a number of petty chiefs. The earliest time at which we can imagine the consolidation to have taken place consistently with what we know of Assyria is about B.C. 760, or nearly half a century later than the date given by Herodotus.

The cause of the sudden growth of Media in power about this period, and of the consolidation which followed rapidly upon that growth, is to be sought, apparently, in fresh migratory movements from the Arian head-quarters, the countries east and south-east of the Caspian. The Cyaxares who about the year B.C. 632 led an invading host of Medes against Nineveh, was so well known to the Arian tribes of the north-east that, when in the reign of Darius Hystaspis a Sagartian raised the standard of revolt in that region he stated the ground of his claim to the Sagartian throne to be descent from Cyaxares. This great chief, it is probable, either alone, or in conjunction with his father (whom Herodotus calls Phraortes), led a fresh emigration of Arians from the Bacterian and Sagartian country to the regions directly east of the Zagros mountain chain; and having thus vastly increased the strength of the Arian race in that quarter, set himself to consolidate a mountain kingdom capable of resisting the great monarchy of the plain. Accepted, it would seem, as chief by the former Arian inhabitants of the tract, he proceeded to reduce the scattered Scythic tribes which had hitherto held possession of the high mountain region. The Zimri, Minni, Hupuska, etc., who divided among them the country lying between Media Proper and Assyria, were attacked and subdued without any great difficulty; and the conqueror, finding himself thus at the head of a considerable kingdom, and no longer in any danger of subjugation at the hands of Assyria, began to contemplate the audacious enterprise of himself attacking the Great Power which had been for so many hundred years the terror of Western Asia. The supineness of Asshur-bani-pal, the Assyrian king, who must at this time have been advanced in years, encouraged his aspirations; and about B.C. 634, when that monarch had held the throne for thirty-four years, suddenly, without warning, the Median troops debouched from the passes of Zagros, and spread themselves over the rich country at its base, Alarmed by the nearness and greatness of the peril, the Assyrian king aroused himself, and putting himself at the head of his troops, marched out to confront the invader. A great battle was fought, probably somewhere in Adiabene, in which the Medes were completely defeated: their whole army was cut to pieces; and the father of Cyaxares was among the slain. Such was the result of the first Median expedition against Nineveh. The assailants had miscalculated their strength. In their own mountain country, and so long as they should be called upon to act only on the defensive, they might be right in regarding themselves as a match for the Assyrians; but when they descended into the plain, and allowed their enemy the opportunity of manoeuvering and of using his war chariots, their inferiority was marked. Cyaxares, now, if not previously, actual king, withdrew awhile from the war, and, convinced that all the valor of his Medes would be unavailing without discipline, set himself to organize the army on a new system, taking a pattern from the enemy, who had long possessed some knowledge of tactics. Hitherto, it would seem, each Median chief had brought into the field his band of followers, some mounted, some on foot, foot and horse alike armed variously as their means allowed them, some with bows and arrows, some with spears, some perhaps with slings or darts; and the army had been composed of a number of such bodies, each chief keeping his band close about him. Cyaxares broke up these bands, and formed the soldiers who composed them into distinct corps, according as they were horsemen or footmen, archers, slingers, or lancers. He then, having completed his arrangements at his ease, without disturbance (so far as appears) from the Assyrians, felt himself strong enough to renew the war with a good prospect of success. Collecting as large an army as he could, both from his Arian and his Scythic subjects, he marched into Assyria, met the troops of Asshur-bani-pal in the field, defeated them signally, and forced them to take refuge behind the strong works which defended their capital. He even ventured to follow up the flying foe and commence the siege of the capital itself; but at this point he was suddenly checked in his career of victory, and forced to assume a defensive attitude, by a danger of a novel kind, which recalled him from Nineveh to his own country.

The vast tracts, chiefly consisting of grassy plains, which lie north of the Black Sea, the Caucasus, the Caspian, and the Jaxartes Syhun river, were inhabited in ancient times by a race or races known to the Asiatics as Saka, "Scythians." These people appear to have been allied ethnically with many of the more southern races, as with the Parthians, the Iberians, the Alarodians, the tribes of the Zagros chain, the Susianians, and others. It is just possible that they may have taken an interest in the warfare of their southern brethren, and that, when Cyaxares brought the tribes of Zagros under his yoke, the Scyths of the north may have felt resentment, or compassion, If this view seem too improbable, considering the distance, the physical obstacles, and the little communication that there was between nations in those early times, we must suppose that by a mere coincidence it happened that the subjugation of the southern Scyths by Cyaxares was followed within a few years by a great irruption of Scyths from the trans-Caucasian region. In that case we shall have to regard the invasion as a mere example of that ever-recurring law by which the poor and hardy races of Upper Asia or Europe are from time to time directed upon the effete kingdoms of the south, to shake, ravage, or overturn them, as the case may be, and prevent them from stagnating into corruption.

The character of the Scythians, and the general nature of their ravages, have been described in a former portion of this work. If they entered Southern Asia, as seems probable, by the Daghestan route, they would then have been able to pass on without much difficulty, through Georgia into Azerbijan, and from Azerbijan into Media Magna, where the Medes had now established their southern capital. Four roads lead from Azerbijan to Hamadan or the Greater Ecbatana, one through Menjil and Kasvin, and across the Caraghan Hills; a second through Miana, Zenjan, and the province of Khamseh; a third by the valley of the Jaghetu, through Chukli and Tikan-Teppeh; and a fourth through Sefer-Khaneh and Sennah. We cannot say which of the four the invaders selected; but, as they were passing southwards, they met the army of Cyaxares, which had quitted Nineveh on the first news of their invasion, and had marched in hot haste to meet and engage them. The two enemies were not ill-matched. Both were hardy and warlike, both active and full of energy; with both the cavalry was the chief arm, and the bow the weapon on which they depended mainly for victory. The Medes were no doubt the better disciplined; they had a greater variety of weapons and of soldiers; and individually they were probably more powerful men than the Scythians; but these last had the advantage of numbers, of reckless daring, and of tactics that it was difficult to encounter. Moreover, the necessity of their situation in the midst of an enemy's country made it imperative on them to succeed, while their adversaries might be defeated without any very grievous consequences. The Scytho had not come into Asia to conquer so much as to ravage; defeat at their hands involved damage rather than destruction; and the Medes must have felt that, if they lost the battle, they might still hope to maintain a stout defence behind the strong walls of some of their towns. The result was such as might have been expected under these circumstances. Madyes, the Scythian leader, obtained the victory, Cyaxares was defeated, and compelled to make terms with the invader. Retaining his royal name, and the actual government of his country, he admitted the suzerainty of the Scyths, and agreed to pay them an annual tribute. Whether Media suffered very seriously from their ravages, we cannot say. Neither its wealth nor its fertility was such as to tempt marauders to remain in it very long. The main complaint made against the Scythian conquerors is that, not content with the fixed tribute which they had agreed to receive, and which was paid them regularly, they levied contributions at their pleasure on the various states under their sway, which were oppressed by repeated exactions. The injuries suffered from their marauding habits form only a subordinate charge against them, as though it had not been practically felt to be so great a grievance. We can well imagine that the bulk of the invaders would prefer the warmer and richer lands of Assyria, Mesopotamia, and Syria; and that, pouring into them, they would leave the colder and less wealthy Media comparatively free from ravage.

The condition of Media and the adjacent countries under the Scythians must have nearly resembled that of almost the same regions under the Seljukian Turks during the early times of their domination. The conquerors made no fixed settlements, but pitched their tents in any portion of the territory that they chose. Their horses and cattle were free to pasture on all lands equally. They were recognized as the dominant race, were feared and shunned, but did not greatly interfere with the bulk of their subjects. It was impossible that they should occupy at any given time more than a comparatively few spots in the wide tract which they had overrun and subjugated; and, consequently, there was not much contact between them and the peoples whom they had conquered. Such contact as there was must no doubt have been galling and oppressive. The right of free pasture in the lands of others is always irksome to those who have to endure it, and, even where it is exercised with strict fairness, naturally leads to quarrels. The barbarous Scythians are not likely to have cared very much about fairness. They would press heavily upon the more fertile tracts, paying over-frequent visits to such spots, and remaining in them till the region was exhausted. The chiefs would not be able to restrain their followers from acts of pillage; redress would be obtained with difficulty; and sometimes even the chiefs themselves may have been sharers in the injuries committed. The insolence, moreover, of a dominant race so coarse and rude as the Scyths must have been very hard to bear; and we can well understand that the various nations which had to endure the yoke must have looked anxiously for an opportunity of shaking it off, and recovering their independence.

Among these various nations, there was probably none that fretted and winced under its subjection more than the Medes. Naturally brave and high-spirited, with the love of independence inherent in mountaineers, and with a well-grounded pride in their recent great successes, they must have chafed daily and hourly at the ignominy of their position, the postponement of their hopes, and the wrongs which they continually suffered. At first it seemed necessary to endure. They had tried the chances of a battle, and had been defeated in fair fight—what reason was there to hope that, if they drew the sword again, they would be more successful? Accordingly they remained quiet but, as time went on, and the Scythians dispersed themselves continually over a wider and a wider space, invading Assyria, Mesopotamia, Syria, Palestine, and again Armenia and Cappadocia, everywhere plundering and marauding, conducting sieges, fighting battles, losing men from the sword, from sickness, from excesses, becoming weaker instead of stronger, as each year went by, owing to the drain of constant wars—the Medes by degrees took heart. Not trusting, however, entirely to the strength of their right arms, a trust which had failed them once, they resolved to prepare the way for an outbreak by a stratagem which they regarded as justifiable. Cyaxares and his court invited a number of the Scythian chiefs to a grand banquet, and, having induced them to drink till they were completely drunk, set upon them when they were in this helpless condition, and remorselessly slew them all.

This deed was the signal for a general revolt of the nation. The Medes everywhere took arms, and, turning upon their conquerors, assailed them with a fury the more terrible because it had been for years repressed. A war followed, the duration and circumstances of which are unknown; for the stories with which Ctesias enlivened this portion of his history can scarcely be accepted as having any foundation in fact. According to him, the Parthians made common cause with the Scythians on the occasion, and the war lasted many years; numerous battles were fought with great loss to both sides; and peace was finally concluded without either party having gained the upper hand. The Scyths were commanded by a queen, Zarina or Zarinsea, woman of rare beauty, and as brave as she was fair; who won the hearts, when she could not resist the swords, of her adversaries. A strangely romantic love-tale is told of this beauteous Amazon. It is not at all clear what region Ctesias supposes her to govern. It has a capital city, called Koxanace (a name entirely unknown to any other historian or geographer), and it contains many other towns of which Zarina was the foundress. Its chief architectural monument was the tomb of Zarina, a triangular pyramid, six hundred feet high, and more than a mile round the base, crowned by a colossal figure of the queen made of solid gold. But—to leave these fables and return to fact—we can only say with certainty that the result of the war was the complete defeat of the Scythians, who not only lost their position of pre-eminence in Media and the adjacent countries, but were driven across the Caucasus into their own proper territory. Their expulsion was so complete that they scarcely left a trace of their power or their presence in the geography or ethnography of the country. One Palestine city only, as already observed, and one Armenian province retained in their names a lingering memory of the great inroad which but for them would have passed away without making any more permanent mark on the region than a hurricane or a snowstorm. How long the dominion of the Scyths endured is a matter of great uncertainty. It was no doubt the belief of Herodotus that from their defeat of Cyaxares to his treacherous murder of their chiefs was a period of exactly twenty-eight years. During the whole of this space he regarded them as the undisputed lords of Asia. It was not till the twenty-eight years were over that the Medes were able, according to him, to renew their attacks on the Assyrians, and once more to besiege Nineveh. But this chronology is open to great objections. There is strong reason for believing that Nineveh fell about B.C. 625 or 624; but according to the numbers of Herodotus the fall would, at the earliest, have taken place in B.C. 602. There is great unlikelihood that the Scyths, if they had maintained their rule for a generation, should not have attracted some distinct notice from the Jewish writers. Again, if twenty-eight out of the forty years assigned to Cyaxares are to be regarded as years of inaction, all his great exploits, his two sieges of Nineveh, his capture of that capital, his conquest of the countries north and west of Media as far as the Halys, his six years' war in Asia Minor beyond that river, and his joint expedition with Nebuchadnezzar into Syria, will have to be crowded most improbably into the space of twelve years, two or three preceding and ten or nine following the Scythian domination. These and other reasons lead to the conclusion, which has the support of Eusebius, that the Scythian domination was of much shorter duration than Herodotus imagined. It may have been twenty-eight years from the original attack on Media to the final expulsion of the last of the invaders from Asia—and this may have been what the informants of Herodotus really intended—but it cannot have been very long after the first attack before the Medes began to recover themselves, to shake off the fear which had possessed them and clear their territories of the invaders. If the invasion really took place in the reign of Cyaxares, and not in the lifetime of his father, where Eusebius places it, we must suppose that within eight years of its occurrence Cyaxares found himself sufficiently strong, and his hands sufficiently free, to resume his old projects, and for the second time to march an army into Assyria.

The weakness of Assyria was such as to offer strong temptations to an invader. As the famous inroad of the Gauls into Italy in the year of Rome 365 paved the way for the Roman conquests in the peninsula by breaking the power of the Etruscans, the Umbrians, and various other races, so the Scythic incursion may have, really benefited, rather than injured, Media, by weakening the great power to whose empire she aspired to succeed. The exhaustion of Assyria's resources at the time is remarkably illustrated by the poverty and meanness of the palace which the last king, Saracus, built for himself at Calah. She lay, apparently, at the mercy of the first bold assailant, her prestige lost, her army dispirited or disorganized, her defences injured, her high spirit broken and subdued.

Cyaxaros, ere proceeding to the attack, sent, it is probable, to make an alliance with the Susianians and Chaldaeans. Susiana was the last country which Assyria had conquered, and could remember the pleasures of independence. Chaldaea, though it had been now for above half a century an Assyrian fief, and had borne the yoke with scarcely a murmur during that period, could never wholly forget its old glories, or the long resistance which it had made before submitting to its northern neighbor. The overtures of the Median monarch seem to have been favorably received; and it was agreed that an army from the south should march up the Tigris and threaten Assyria from that quarter, while Cyaxares led his Medes from the east, through the passes of Zagros against the capital. Rumor soon conveyed the tidings of his enemies' intentions to the Assyrian monarch, who immediately made such a disposition of the forces at his command as seemed best calculated to meet the double danger which threatened him. Selecting from among his generals the one in whom he placed most confidence—a man named Nabopolassar, most probably an Assyrian—he put him at the head of a portion of his troops, and sent him to Babylon to resist the enemy who was advancing from the sea. The command of his main army he reserved for himself, intending to undertake in person the defence of his territory against the Medes. This plan of campaign was not badly conceived; but it was frustrated by an unexpected calamity. Nabopolassar, seeing his sovereign's danger, and calculating astutely that he might gain more by an opportune defection from a falling cause than he could look to receive as the reward of fidelity, resolved to turn traitor and join the enemies of Assyria. Accordingly he sent an embassy to Cyaxares, with proposals for a close alliance to be cemented by a marriage. If the Median monarch would give his daughter Amuhia (or Amyitis) to be the wife of his son Nebuchadnezzar, the forces under his command should march against Nineveh and assist Cyaxares to capture it. Such a proposition arriving at such a time was not likely to meet with a refusal. Cyaxares gladly came into the terms; the marriage took place; and Nabopolassar, who had now practically assumed the sovereignty of Babylon, either led or sent a Babylonian contingent to the aid of the Medes.

The siege of Nineveh by the combined Medes and Babylonians was narrated by Ctesias at some length. He called the Assyrian king Sardanapalus, the Median commander Arbaces, the Babylonian Belesis. Though he thus disguised the real names, and threw back the event to a period a century and a half earlier than its true date, there can be no doubt that he intended to relate the last siege of the city, that which immediately preceded its complete destruction. He told how the combined army, consisting of Persians and Arabs as well as of Medes and Babylonians, and amounting to four hundred thousand men, was twice defeated with great loss by the Assyrian monarch, and compelled to take refuge in the Zagros chain—how after losing a third battle it retreated to Babylonia—how it was there joined by strong reinforcements from Bactria, surprised the Assyrian camp by night, and drove the whole host in confusion to Nineveh—how then, after two more victories, it advanced and invested the city, which was well provisioned for a siege and strongly fortified. The siege, Ctesias said, had lasted two full years, and the third year had commenced—success seemed still far off—when an unusually rainy season so swelled the waters of the Tigris that they burst into the city, sweeping away more than two miles of the wall. This vast breach it was impossible to repair; and the Assyrian monarch, seeing that further resistance was vain, brought the struggle to an end by burning himself, with his concubines and eunuchs and all his chief wealth, in his palace.

Such, in outline, was the story of Ctesias. If we except the extent of the breach which the river is declared to have made, it contains no glaring improbabilities. On the contrary, it is a narrative that hangs well together, and that suits both the relations of the parties and the localities. Moreover, it is confirmed in one or two points by authorities of the highest order. Still, as Ctesias is a writer who delights in fiction, and as it seems very unlikely that he would find a detailed account of the siege, such as he has given us, in the Persian archives, from whence he professed to derive his history, no confidence can be placed in those points of his narrative which have not any further sanction. All that we know on the subject of the last siege of Nineveh is that it was conducted by a combined army of Medes and Babylonians, the former commanded by Cyaxares, the latter by Nabopolassar or

Nebuchadnezzar, and that it was terminated, when all hope was lost, by the suicide of the Assyrian monarch. The self-immolation of Saracus is related by Abydenus, who almost certainly follows Berosus in this part of his history. We may therefore accept it as a fact about which there ought to be no question. Actuated by a feeling which has more than once caused a vanquished monarch to die rather than fall into the power of his enemies, Saracus made a funeral pyre of his ancestral palace, and lighted it with his own hand.

One further point in the narrative of Ctesias we may suspect to contain a true representation. Ctesias declared the cause of the capture to have been the destruction of the city wall by an unexpected rise of the river. Now, the prophet Nahum, in his announcement of the fate coming on Nineveh, has a very remarkable expression, which seems most naturally to point to some destruction of a portion of the fortifications by means of water. After relating the steps that would be taken for the defence of the place, he turns to remark on their fruitlessness, and says: "The gates of the rivers are opened, and the palace is dissolved; and Huzzab is led away captive; she is led up, with her maidens, sighing as with the voice of doves, smiting upon their breasts." Now, we have already seen that at the northwest angle of Nineveh there was a sluice or floodgate, intended mainly to keep the water of the Khosrsu, which ordinarily filled the city moat, from flowing off too rapidly into the Tigris, but probably intended also to keep back the water of the Tigris, when that stream rose above its common level. A sudden and great rise of the Tigris would necessarily endanger this gate, and if it gave way beneath the pressure, a vast torrent of water would rush up the moat along and against the northern wall, which may have been undermined by its force, and have fallen in. The stream would then pour into the city; and it may perhaps have reached the palace platform, which being made of sun-dried bricks, and probably not cased with stone inside the city, would begin to be "dissolved." Such seems the simplest and best interpretation of this passage, which, though it is not historical, but only prophetical, must be regarded as giving an importance that it would not otherwise have possessed to the statement of Ctesias with regard to the part played by the Tigris in the destruction of Nineveh.

The fall of the city was followed by a division of the spoil between the two principal conquerors. While Cyaxares took to his own share the land of the conquered people, Assyria Proper, and the countries dependent on Assyria towards the north and north-west, Nabopolassar was allowed, not merely Babylonia, Chaldaea, and Susiana, but the valley of the Euphrates and the countries to which that valley conducted. Thus two considerable empires arose at the same time cut of the ashes of Assyria—the Babylonian towards the south and the south-west, stretching from Luristan to the borders of Egypt, the Median towards the north, reaching from the salt desert of Iran to Amanus and the Upper Euphrates. These empires were established by mutual consent; they were connected together, not merely by treaties, but by the ties of affinity which united their rulers; and, instead of cherishing, as might have been expected, a mutual suspicion and distrust, they seem to have really entertained the most friendly feelings towards one another, and to have been ready on all emergencies to lend each other important assistance. For once in the history of the world two powerful monarchies were seen to stand side by side, not only without collision, but without jealousy or rancor. Babylonia and Media were content to share between them the empire of Western Asia: the world was, they thought, wide enough for both; and so, though they could not but have had in some respects conflicting interests, they remained close friends and allies for more than half a century.

To the Median monarch the conquest of Assyria did not bring a time of repose. Wandering bands of Scythians were still, it is probable, committing ravages in many parts of Western Asia. The subjects of Assyria, set free by her downfall, were likely to use the occasion for the assertion of their independence, if they were not immediately shown that a power of at least equal strength had taken her place, and was prepared to claim her inheritance. War begets war; and the successes of Cyaxares up to the present point in his career did but whet his appetite for power, and stimulate him to attempt further conquests. In brief but pregnant words Herodotus informs us that Cyaxares "subdued to himself all Asia above the

Halys." How much he may include in this expression, it is impossible to determine; but, prime facie, it would seem at least to imply that he engaged in a series of wars with the various tribes and nations which intervened between Media and Assyria on the one side and the river Halys on the other, and that he succeeded in bringing them under his dominion. The most important countries in this direction were Armenia and Cappadocia. Armenia, strong in its lofty mountains, its deep gorges, and its numerous rapid rivers—the head-streams of the Tigris, Euphrates, Kur, and Aras—had for centuries resisted with unconquered spirit the perpetual efforts of the Assyrian kings to bring it under their yoke, and had only at last consented under the latest king but one to a mere nominal allegiance. Cappadocia had not even been brought to this degree of dependence. It had lain beyond the furthest limit whereto the Assyrian arms had ever reached, and had not as yet come into collision with any of the great powers of Asia. Other minor tribes in this region, neighbors of the Armenians and Cappadocians, but more remote from Media, were the Ibenans, the Colchians, the Moschi, the Tibareni, the Mares the Macrones, and the Mosynoeci. Herodotus appears to have been of opinion that all these tribes, or at any rate all but the Colchians, were at this time brought under by Cyaxares who thus extended his dominions to the Caucasus and the Black Sea upon the north, and upon the east to the Kizil Irmak or Halys.

It is possible that the reduction of these countries under the Median yoke was not so much a conquest as a voluntary submission of the inhabitants to the power which alone seemed strong enough to save them from the hated domination of the Scyths. According to Strabo, Armenia and Cappadocia were the regions where the Scythic ravages had been most severely felt. Cappadocia had been devastated from the mountains down to the coast; and in Armenia the most fertile portion of the whole territory had been seized and occupied by the invaders, from whom it thenceforth took the name of Sacassene, the Armenians and Cappadocians may have found the yoke of the Scyths so intolerable as to have gladly exchanged it for dependence on a comparatively civilized people. In the neighboring territory of Asia Minor a similar cause had recently exercised a unifying influence, the necessity of combining to resist Cimmerian immigrants having tended to establish a hegemony of Lydia over the various tribes which divided among them the tract west of the Halys. It is evidently not improbable that the sufferings endured at the hands of the Scyths may have disposed the nations east of the river to adopt the same remedy and that, so soon as Media had proved her strength, first by shaking herself free of the Scythic invaders and then conquering Assyria. the tribes of these parts accepted her as at once their mistress and their deliverer.

Another quite distinct cause may also have helped to bring about the result above indicated. Parallel with the great Median migration from the East under Cyaxares, or Phraortes (?), his father, an Arian influx had taken place into the countries between the Caspian and the Halys. In Armenia and Cappadocia during the flourishing period of Assyria, Turanian tribes had been predominant. Between the middle and the end of the seventh century these tribes appear to have yielded the supremacy to Arians. In Armenia, the present language which is predominantly Arian, ousted the former Turaman tongue which appears in the cuneiform inscriptions of Van and the adjacent regions. In Cappadocia, the Moschi and Tibareni had to yield their seats to a new race—the Katapatuka, who were not only Arian but distinctly Medo-Persic, as is plain from their proper names, and from the close connection of their royal house with that of the kings of Persia. This spread of the Arians into the countries lying between the Caspian and the Halys must have done much to pave the way for Median supremacy over those regions. The weaker Arian tribes of the north would have been proud of their southern brethren, to whose arms the queen of Western Asia had been forced to yield, and would have felt comparatively little repugnance in surrendering their independence into the hands of a friendly and kindred people.

Thus Cyaxares, in his triumphant progress to the north and the north-west, made war, it is probable, chiefly upon the Scyths, or upon them and the old Turanian inhabitants of the countries, while by the Arians he was welcomed as a champion come to deliver them from a grievous oppression. Ranging themselves under his standard, they probably helped him to expel from Asia the barbarian hordes which had now for many years tyrannized over them; and when the expulsion was completed, gratitude or habit made them willing to continue in the subject position which they had assumed in order to effect it. Cyaxares within less than ten years from his capture of Nineveh had added to his empire the fertile and valuable tracts of Armenia and Cappadocia—never really subject to Assyria—and may perhaps have further mastered the entire region between Armenia and the Caucasus and Euxine.

The advance of their western frontier to the river Halys, which was involved in the absorption of Cappadocia into the Empire, brought the Medes into contact with a new power—a power which, like Media, had been recently increasing in greatness, and which was not likely to submit to a foreign yoke without a struggle. The Lydian kingdom was one of great antiquity in this part of Asia. According to traditions current among its people, it had been established more than seven hundred years at the time when Cyaxares pushed his conquests to its borders. Three dynasties of native kings—Atyadse, Heraclidse, and Mermnadae—had successively held the throne during that period. The Lydians could repeat the names of at least thirty monarchs who had borne sway in Sardis, their capital city, since its foundation. They had never been conquered. In the old times, indeed, Lydus, the son of Atys, had changed the name of the people inhabiting the country from Maeonians to Lydians—a change which to the keen sense of an historical critic implies a conquest of one race by another. But to the people themselves this tradition conveyed no such meaning; or, if it did to any, their self-complacency was not disturbed thereby, since they would hug the notion that they belonged not to the conquered race but to the conquerors. If a Ramcsos or a Sesostris had ever penetrated to their country, he had met with a brave resistance, and had left monuments indicating his respect for their courage. Neither Babylon nor Assyria had ever given a king to the Lydians—on the contrary, the Lydian tradition was, that they had themselves sent forth Belus and Ninus from their own country to found dynasties and cities in Mesopotamia. In a still more remote age they had seen their colonists embark upon the western waters, and start for the distant Hesperia, where they had arrived in safety, and had founded the great Etruscan nation. On another occasion they had carried their arms beyond the limits of Asia Minor, and had marched southward to the very extremity of: Syria, where their general, Ascalus, had founded a great city and called it after his name.

Such were the Lydian traditions with respect to the more remote times. Of their real history they seem to have known but little, and that little did not extend further back than about two hundred years before Cyaxares. Within this space it was certain that they had had a change of dynasty, a change preceded by a long feud between their two greatest houses, which were perhaps really two branches of the royal family. The Heraclidae had grown jealous of the Mermnadae, and had treated them with injustice; the Mormnadae had at first sought their safety in flight, and afterwards, when they felt themselves strong enough, had returned, murdered the Heraclide monarch, and placed their chief, Gyges, upon the throne. With Gyges, who had commenced his reign about B.C. 700, the prosperity of the Lydians had greatly increased, and they had begun to assume an aggressive attitude towards their neighbors. Gyges' revenue was so great that his wealth became proverbial, and he could afford to spread his fame by sending from his superfluity to the distant temple of Delphi presents of such magnificence that they were the admiration of later ages. The relations of his predecessors with the Greeks of the Asiatic coast had been friendly, Gyges changed this policy, and, desirous of enlarging his seaboard, made war upon the Greek maritime towns, attacking Miletus and Smyrna without result, but succeeding in capturing the Ionic city of Colophon. He also picked a quarrel with the inland town of Magnesia, and after many invasions of its territory compelled it to submission. According to some, he made himself master of the whole territory of the Troad, and the Milesians had to obtain his permission before they could establish their colony of Abydos upon the Hellespont. At any rate he was a rich and puissant monarch in the eyes of the Greeks of Asia and the islands, who were never tired of celebrating his wealth, his wars, and his romantic history.

The shadow of calamity had, however, fallen upon Lydia towards the close of Gyges' long reign. About thirty years before the Scythians from the Steppe country crossed the Caucasus and fell upon Media, the same barrier was passed by another groat horde of nomads. The Cimmerians, probably a Celtic people, who had dwelt hitherto in the Tauric Chersonese and the country adjoining upon it, pressed on by Scythic invaders from the East, had sought a vent in this direction. Passing the great mountain barrier either by the route of Mozdok—the Pylas Caucasiae—or by some still more difficult track towards the Euxine, they had entered Asia Minor by way of Cappadocia and had spread terror and devastation in every direction. Gyges, alarmed at their advance, had placed himself under the protection of Assyria, and had then confidently given them battle, defeated them, and captured several of their chiefs. It is uncertain whether the Assyrians gave him any material aid, but evident that he ascribed his success to his alliance with them. In his gratitude he sent an embassy to Asshur-bani-pal, king of Assyria, and courted his favor by presents and by sending him his Cimmerian captives. Later in his reign, however, he changed his policy, and, breaking with Assyria, gave aid to the Egyptian rebel, Psammetichus, and helped him to establish his independence. The result followed which was to be expected. Assyria withdrew her protection; and Lydia was left to fight her own battles when the great crisis came. Carrying all before them, the fierce hordes swarmed in full force into the more western districts of Asia Minor; Paphlagonia, Phrygia, Bithynia, Lydia, and Ionia were overrun; Gyges, venturing on an engagement, perished; the frightened inhabitants generally shut themselves up in their walled towns, and hoped that the tide of invasion might sweep by them quickly and roll elsewhere; but the Cimmerians, impatient and undisciplined as they might be, could sometimes bring themselves to endure the weary work of a siege, and they saw in the Lydian capital a prize well worth an effort. The hordes besieged Sardis, and took it, except the citadel, which was commandingly placed and defied all their attempts. A terrible scene of carnage must have followed. How Lydia withstood the blow, and rapidly recovered from it, is hard to understand; but it seems certain that within a generation she was so far restored to vigor as to venture on resuming her attacks upon the Greeks of the coast, which had been suspended during her period of prostration. Sadyattes, the son of Ardys, and grandson of Gyges, following the example of his father and grandfather, made war upon Miletus; and Alyattes, his son and successor, pursued the same policy of aggression. Besides pressing Miletus, he besieged and took Smyrna, and ravaged the territory of Clazomenae.

But the great work of Alyattes' reign, and the one which seems to have had the most important consequences for Lydia, was the war which he undertook for the purpose of expelling the Cimmerians from Asia Minor. The hordes had been greatly weakened by time, by their losses in war, and, probably by their excesses; they had long ceased to be formidable; but they were still strong enough to be an annoyance. Alyattes is said to have "driven them out of Asia," by which we can scarcely understand less than that he expelled them from his own dominions and those of his neighbors—or, in other words, from the countries which had been the scenes of their chief ravages—Paphlagonia, Bithynia, Lydia, Phrygia, and Cilicia. But, to do this, he must have entered into a league with his neighbors, who must have consented to act under him for the purposes of war, if they did not even admit the permanent hegemony of his country. Alyattes' success appears to have been complete, or nearly so; he cleared Asia Minor of the Cimmerians; and having thus conferred a benefit on all the nations of the region and exhibited before their eyes his great military capacity, if he had not actually constructed an empire, he had at any rate done much to pave the way for one.

Such was the political position in the regions west and south of the Halys, when Cyaxares completed his absorption of Cappadocia, and looking across the river that divided the Cappadocians from the Phrygians, saw stretched before him a region of great fertile plains, which seemed to invite an invader. A pretext for an attack was all that he wanted, and this was soon forthcoming. A body of the nomad Scyths—probably belonging to the great invasion, though Herodotus thought otherwise—had taken service under Cyaxares, and for some time served him faithfully, being employed chiefly as hunters. A cause of quarrel, however, arose after a while; and the Scyths, disliking their position or distrusting the intentions of their lords towards them, quitted the Median territory, and, marching through a great part of Asia Minor, sought and found a refuge with Alyattes, the Lydian king. Cyaxares, upon learning their flight, sent an embassy to the court of Sardis to demand the surrender of the fugitives; but the Lydian monarch met the demand with a refusal, and, fully understanding the probable consequences, immediately prepared for war.

Though Lydia, compared to Media, was but a small state, yet her resources were by no means inconsiderable. In fertility she surpassed almost every other country of Asia Minor, which is altogether one of the richest regions in the world. At this time she was producing large quantities of gold, which was found in great abundance in the Pactolus, and probably in the other small streams that flowed down on all sides from the Tmolus mountain-chain. Her people were at once warlike and ingenious. They had invented the art of coining money, and showed considerable taste in their devices. [PLATE VII., Fig. 1], They claimed also to have been the inventors of a number of games, which were common to them with the Greeks. According to Herodotus, they were the first who made a livelihood by shop-keeping. They were skilful in the use of musical instruments, and had their own peculiar musical mode or style, which was in much favor among the Greeks, though condemned as effeminate by some of the philosophers. At the same time the Lydians were not wanting in courage or manliness. They fought chiefly on horseback, and were excellent riders, carrying long spears, which they managed with great skill. Nicolas of Damascus tells us that even under the Heraclido kings, they could muster for service cavalry to the number of 30,000. In peace they pursued with ardor the sports of the field, and found in the chase of the wild boar a pastime which called forth and exercised every manly quality. Thus Lydia, even by herself, was no contemptible enemy; though it can hardly be supposed that, without help from others, she would have proved a match for the Great Median Empire.

But such help as she needed was not wanting to her. The rapid strides with which Media had advanced towards the west had no doubt alarmed the numerous princes of Asia Minor, who must have felt that they had a power to deal with as full of schemes of conquest as Assyria, and more capable of carrying her designs into execution. It has been already observed that the long course of Assyrian aggressions developed gradually among the Asiatic tribes a tendency to unite in leagues for purposes of resistance. The circumstances of the time called now imperatively for such a league to be formed, unless the princes of Asia Minor were content to have their several territories absorbed one after another into the growing Median Empire. These princes appear to have seen their danger. Cyaxares may perhaps have, declared war specially against the Lydians, and have crossed the Halys professedly in order to chastise them; but he could only reach Lydia through the territories of other nations, which he was evidently intending to conquer on his way; and it was thus apparent that he was activated, not by anger against a particular power, but by a general design of extending his dominions in this direction. A league seems therefore to have been determined on. We have not indeed any positive evidence of its existence till the close of the war; but the probabilities are wholly in favor of its having taken effect from the first. Prudence would have dictated such a course; and it seems almost implied in the fact that a successful resistance was made to the Median attack from the very commencement. We may conclude therefore that the princes of Asia Minor, having either met in conclave or communicated by embassies, resolved to make common cause, if the Medes crossed the Halys; and that, having already acted under Lydia in the expulsion of the Cimmerians from their territories, they naturally placed her at their head when they coalesced for the second time.

Fig. 1.

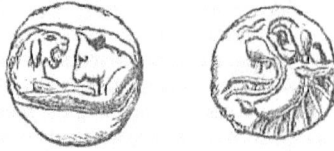

No. 1.   No. 2.

Lydian Coins.

Fig. 2.

View of the Lebanon range.

Fig. 3.

Hare sitting, from a Babylonian
cylinder.

Hare carried in the hands, from
a Babylonian cylinder.

PLATE VII

Cyaxares on his part, was not content to bring against the confederates merely the power of Media. He requested and obtained a contingent from the Babylonian monarch, Nabopolassar, and may not improbably have had the assistance of other allies also. With a vast army drawn from various parts of inner Asia, he invaded the territory of the Western Powers, and began his attempt at subjugation. We have no detailed account of the war; but we learn from the general expressions of Herodotus that the Median monarch met with a most stubborn resistance; numerous engagements were fought with varied results; sometimes the Medes succeeded in defeating their adversaries in pitched battles; but sometimes, and apparently as often, the Lydians and their allies gained decided victories over the Medes. It is noted that one of the engagements took place by night, a rare occurrence in ancient (as in modern) times. The war had continued six years, and the Medes had evidently made no serious impression, when a remarkable circumstance brought it suddenly to a termination. The two armies had once more met and were engaged in conflict, when, in the midst of the struggle, an ominous darkness fell upon the combatants and filled them with superstitious awe. The sun was eclipsed, either totally or at any rate considerably, so that the attention of the two armies was attracted to it; and, discontinuing the fight, they stood to gaze at the phenomenon. In most parts of the East such an occurrence is even now seen with dread—the ignorant mass believe that the orb of day is actually being devoured or destroyed, and that the end of all things is at hand—even the chiefs, who may have some notion that the phenomenon is a recurrent one, do not understand its cause, and participate in the alarm of their followers. On the present occasion it is said that, amid the general fear, a desire for reconciliation seized both armies. Of this spontaneous movement two chiefs, the foremost of the allies on either side, took advantage. Syennesis, king of Cilicia, the first known monarch of his name, on the part of Lydia, and a prince whom Herodotus calls "Labynetus of Babylon"—probably either Nabopolassar or Nebuchadnezzar—on the part of Media, came forward to propose an immediate armistice; and, when the proposal was accepted on either side, proceeded to the more difficult task of arranging terms of peace between the contending parties. Since nothing is said of the Scythians, who had been put forward as the ostensible grounds of quarrel, we may presume that Alyattes retained them. It is further clear that both he and his allies preserved undiminished both their territories and their independence. The territorial basis of the treaty was thus what in modern diplomatic language is called the status quo; matters, in other words, returned to the position in which they had stood before the war broke out. The only difference was that Cyaxares gained a friend and an ally where he had previously had a jealous enemy; since it was agreed that the two kings of Media and Lydia should swear a friendship, and that, to cement the alliance, Alyattes should give his daughter Aryenis in marriage to Astyages, the son of Cyaxares. The marriage thus arranged took place soon afterwards, while the oath of friendship was sworn at once. According to the barbarous usages of the time and place, the two monarchs, having met and repeated the words of the formula, punctured their own arms, and then sealed their contract by each sucking from the wound a portion of the other's blood.

By this peace the three great monarchies of the time—the Median, the Lydian, and the Babylonian—were placed on terms, not only of amity, but of intimacy and (if the word may be used) of blood relationship. The Crown Princes of the three kingdoms had become brothers. From the shores of the Aegean to those of the Persian Gulf, Western Asia was now ruled by interconnected dynasties, bound by treaties to respect each other's rights, and perhaps to lend each other aid in important conjunctures, and animated, it would seem, by a real spirit of mutual friendliness and attachment. After more than five centuries of almost constant war and ravage, after fifty years of fearful strife and convulsion, during which the old monarchy of Assyria had gone down and a new Empire—the Median—had risen up in its place, this part of Asia entered upon a period of repose which stands out in strong contrast with the long term of struggle. From the date of the peace between Alyattes and Cyaxares (probably B.C. 610), for nearly half a century, the three kingdoms of Media, Lydia, and Babylonia remained fast friends, pursuing their separate courses without quarrel or collision, and thus giving to the nations within their borders a rest and a refreshment which they must have greatly needed and desired.

In one quarter only was this rest for a short time disturbed. During the troublous period the neighboring country of Egypt, which had recovered its freedom, and witnessed a revival of its ancient prosperity, under the Psamatik family, began once more to aspire to the possession of those provinces which, being divided off from the rest of the Asiatic continent by the impassable Syrian desert, seems politically to belong to Africa almost more than to Asia. Psamatik I., the Psammetichus of Herodotus, had commenced an aggressive war in this quarter, probably about the time that Assyria was suffering from the Median and then from the Scythian inroads. He had besieged for several years the strong Philistine town of Ashdod, which commands the coast-route from Egypt to Palestine, and was at this time a most important city. Despite a resistance which would have wearied out any less pertinacious assailant, he had persevered in his attempt, and had finally succeeded in taking the place. He had thus obtained a firm footing in Syria; and his successor was, able, starting from this vantage-ground, to overrun and conquer the whole territory. About the year B.C. 608, Neco, son of Psamatik I., having recently ascended the throne, invaded Palestine with a large army, met and defeated Josiah, king of Judah, near Megiddo in the great plain of Esdraelon, and, pressing forward through Syria to the Euphrates, attacked and took Carchemish, the strong city which guarded the ordinary passage of the river. Idumea, Palestine, Phoenicia, and Syria submitted to him, and for three years he remained in undisturbed possession of his conquest. Then, however, the Babylonians, who had received these provinces at the division of the Assyrian Empire, began to bestir themselves. Nebuchadnezzar marched to Carchemish, defeated the army of Neco, recovered all the territory to the border of Egypt, and even ravaged a portion of that country. It is probable that in this expedition he was assisted by the Medes. At any rate, seven or eight years afterwards, when the intrigues of Egypt had again created disturbances in this quarter, and Jehoiakim, the Jewish king, broke into open insurrection, the Median monarch sent a contingent, which accompanied Nebuchadnezzar into Judaea, and assisted him to establish his power firmly in South-Western Asia.

This is the last act that we can ascribe to the great Median king. He can scarcely have been much less than seventy years old at this time; and his life was prolonged at the utmost three years longer. According to Herodotus, he died B.C. 593, after a reign of exactly forty years, leaving his crown to his son Astyages, whose marriage with a Lydian princess was above related.

We have no sufficient materials from which to draw out a complete character of Cyaxares. He appears to have possessed great ambition, considerable military ability, and a rare tenacity of purpose, which gained him his chief successes. At the same time he was not wanting in good sense, and could bring himself to withdraw from an enterprise, when he had misjudged the fitting time for it, or greatly miscalculated its difficulties. He was faithful to his friends, but thought treachery allowable towards his enemies. He knew how to conquer, but not how to organize, an empire; and, if we except his establishment of Magism, as the religion of the state, we may say that he did nothing to give permanency to the monarchy which he founded. He was a conqueror altogether after the Asiatic model, able to wield the sword, but not to guide the pen, to subdue his contemporaries to his will by his personal ascendency over them, but not to influence posterity by the establishment of a kingdom, or of institutions, on deep and stable foundations. The Empire, which owed to him its foundation, was the most shortlived of all the great Oriental monarchies, having begun and ended within the narrow space of three score and ten years—the natural lifetime of an individual.

Astyages, who succeeded to the Median throne about B.C. 593, had neither his father's enterprise nor his ability. Born to an empire, and bred up in all the luxury of an Oriental Court, he seems to have been quite content with the lot which fortune appeared to have assigned him, and to have coveted no grander position. Tradition says that he was remarkably handsome, cautious, and of an easy and generous temper. Although the anecdotes related of his mode of life at Ecbatana by Herodotus, Xenophon, and Nicolas of Damascus, seem to be for the most part apocryphal, and at any rate come to us upon authority too weak to entitle them to a place in history, we may perhaps gather from the concurrent, descriptions of these three writers something of the general character of the Court over which he presided. Its leading features do not seem to have differed greatly from those of the Court of Assyria. The monarch lived secluded, and could only be seen by those who asked and obtained an audience. He was surrounded by guards and eunuchs, the latter of whom held most of the offices near the royal person. The Court was magnificent in its apparel, in its banquets, and in the number and organization of its attendants. The courtiers wore long flowing robes of many different colors, amongst which red and purple predominated, and adorned their necks with chains or collars of gold, and their wrists with bracelets of the same precious metal. Even the horses on which they rode had sometimes golden bits to their bridles. One officer of the Court was especially called "the King's Eye;" another had the privilege of introducing strangers to him; a third was his cupbearer; a fourth his messenger. Guards torch-bearers, serving-men, ushers, and sweepers, were among the orders into which the lower sort of attendants were divided; while among the courtiers of the highest rank was a privileged class known as "the King's table-companions". The chief pastime in which the Court indulged was hunting. Generally this took place in a park or "paradise" near the capital; but sometimes the King and Court went out on a grand hunt into the open country, where lions, leopards, bears, wild boars, wild asses, antelopes, stags, and wild sheep abounded, and, when the beasts had been driven by beaters into a confined space, despatched them with arrows and javelins.

Prominent at the Court, according to Herodotus, was the priestly caste of the Magi. Held in the highest honor by both King and people, they were in constant attendance, ready to expound omens or dreams, and to give their advice on all matters of state policy. The religious ceremonial was, as a matter of course, under their charge; and it is probable that high state offices were often conferred upon them. Of all classes of the people they were the only one that could feel they had a real influence over the monarch, and might claim to share in his sovereignty.

The long reign of Astyages seems to have been almost undisturbed, until just before its close, by wars or rebellions. Eusebius indeed relates that he, and not Cyaxares, carried on the great Lydian contest; and Moses of Chorene declares that he was engaged in a long struggle with Tigranes, an Armenian king. But little credit can be attached to these statements, the former of which contradicts Herodotus, while the latter is wholly unsupported by any other writer. The character which Cyaxares bore among the Greeks was evidently that of an unwarlike king. If he had really carried his arms into the heart of Asia Minor, and threatened the whole of that extensive region with subjugation, we can scarcely suppose that he would have been considered so peaceful a ruler. Neither is it easy to imagine that in that case no classical writer—not even Ctesias—would have taxed Herodotus with an error that must have been so flagrant. With respect to the war with Tigranes, it is just possible that it may have a basis of truth; there may have been a revolt of Armenia from Astyages under a certain Tigranes, followed by an attempt at subjugation. But the slender authority of Moses is insufficient to establish the truth of his story, which is internally improbable and quite incompatible with the narrative of Herodotus.

There are some grounds for believing that in one direction Astyages succeeded in slightly extending the limits of his empire. But he owed his success to prudent management, and not to courage or military skill. On the north-eastern frontier, occupying the low country now known as Talish and Ghilan, was a powerful tribe called Cadusians, probably of Arian origin, which had hitherto maintained its independence. This would not be surprising, if we could accept the statement of Diodorus that they were able to bring into the field 200,000 men. But this account, which probably came from Ctesias, and is wholly without corroboration from other writers, has the air of a gross exaggeration; and we may conclude from the general tenor of ancient history that the Cadusians were more indebted to the strength of their country, than to either their numbers or their prowess, for the freedom and independence which they were still enjoying. It seems that they were at this time under the government of a certain king, or chief, named Aphernes, or Onaphernes. This ruler was, it appears, doubtful of his position, and, thinking it could not be long maintained, made overtures of surrender to Astyages, which were gladly entertained by that monarch. A secret treaty was concluded to the satisfaction of both parties; and the Cadusians, it would seem, passed under the Medes by this arrangement, without any hostile struggle, though armed resistance on the part of the people, who were ignorant of the intentions of their chieftain, was for some time apprehended.

The domestic relations of Astyages seem to have been unhappy. His "marriage de convenance" with the Lydian princess Aryenis, if not wholly unfruitful, at any rate brought him no son; and, as he grew to old age, the absence of such support to the throne must have been felt very sensibly, and have caused great uneasiness. The want of an heir perhaps led him to contract those other marriages of which we hear in the Armenian History of Moses—one with a certain Anusia, of whom nothing more is known; and another with an Armenian princess, the loveliest of her sex, Tigrania, sister of the Armenian king, Tigranes. The blessing of male offspring was still, however, denied him; and it is even doubtful whether he was really the father of any daughter or daughters. Herodotus, and Xenophon, indeed give him a daughter Mandane, whom they make the mother of Cyrus; and Ctesias, who denied in the most positive terms the truth of this statement, gave him a daughter, Amytis, whom he made the wife, first of Spitaces the Mede, and afterwards of Cyrus the Persian. But these stories, which seem intended to gratify the vanity of the Persians by tracing the descent of their kings to the great Median conqueror, while at the same time they flattered the Medes by showing them that the issue of their old monarchs was still seated on the Arian throne, are entitled to little more credit than the narrative of the Shahnameh, which declares that Iskander (Alexander) was the son of Darab (Darius) and of a daughter of Failakus (Philip of Macedon). When an oriental crown passes from one dynasty to another, however foreign and unconnected, the natives are wont to invent a relationship between the two houses, which both parties are commonly quite ready to accept; as it suits the rising house to be provided with a royal ancestry, and it pleases the fallen one and its partisans to see in the occupants of the throne a branch of the ancient stock—a continuation of the legitimate family. Tales therefore of the above-mentioned kind are, historically speaking, valueless; and it must remain uncertain whether the second Median monarch had any child at all, either male or female.

Old age was now creeping upon the sonless king. If he was sixteen or seventeen years old at the time of his contract of marriage with Aryenis, he must have been nearly seventy in B.C. 558, when the revolt occurred which terminated both his reign and his kingdom. It appears that the Persian branch of the Arian race, which had made itself a home in the country lying south and south-east of Media, between the 32nd parallel and the Persian gulf, had acknowledged some subjection to the Median kings during the time of their greatness. Dwelling in their rugged mountains and high upland plains, they had however maintained the simplicity of their primitive manners, and had mixed but little with the Medes, being governed by their own native princes of the Achasmenian house, the descendants, real or supposed, of a certain Achajmenes. These princes were connected by marriage with the Cappadocian kings; and their house was regarded as one of the noblest in Western Asia. What the exact terms were upon which they stood with the Median monarch is uncertain. Herodotus regards Persia as absorbed into Media at this time, and the Achsemenidse as merely a good Persian family. Nicolas of Damascus makes Persia a Median satrapy, of which Atradates, the father of Cyrus, is satrap, Xenophon, on the contrary, not only gives the Achajmenidae their royal rank, but seems to consider Persia as completely independent of Media; Moses of Chorene takes the same view, regarding Cyrus as a great and powerful sovereign during the reign of Astyages. The native records lean towards the view of Xenophon and Moses. Darius declares that eight of his race had been kings before himself, and makes no difference between his own royalty and theirs. Cyrus calls himself in one inscription "the son of Cambyses, the powerful king." It is certain therefore that Persia continued to be ruled by her own native monarchs during the whole of the Median period, and that Cyrus led the attack upon Astyages as hereditary Persian king. The Persian records seem rather to imply actual independence of Media; but as national vanity would prompt to dissimulation in such a case, we may perhaps accord so much weight to the statement of Herodotus, and to the general tradition on the subject, as to believe that there was some kind of acknowledgment of Median supremacy on the part of the Persian kings anterior to Cyrus, though the acknowledgment may have been not much more than a formality and have imposed no onerous obligations. The residence of Cyrus at the Median Court, which is asserted in almost every narrative of his life before he became king, inexplicable if Persia was independent, becomes thoroughly intelligible on the supposition that she was a great Median feudatory. In such cases the residence of the Crown Prince at the capital of the suzerain is constantly desired, or even required by the superior Power, which sees in the presence of the son and heir the best security against disaffection or rebellion on the part of the father.

It appears that Cyrus, while at the Median Court, observing the unwarlike temper of the existing generation of the Medes, who had not seen any actual service, and despising the personal character of the monarch, who led a luxurious life, chiefly at Ecbatana, amid eunuchs, concubines, and dancing-girls, resolved on raising the standard of rebellion, and seeking at any rate to free his own country. It may be suspected that the Persian prince was not actuated solely by political motives. To earnest Zoroastrians, such as the Achgemenians are shown to have been by their inscriptions, the yoke of a Power which had so greatly corrupted, if it had not wholly laid aside, the worship of Ormazd, must have been extremely distasteful; and Cyrus may have wished by his rebellion as much to vindicate the honor of his religion— as to obtain a loftier position for his nation. If the Magi occupied really the position at the Median Court which Herodotus assigns to them—if they "were held in high honor by the king, and shared in his sovereignty"—if the priest-ridden monarch was perpetually dreaming and perpetually referring his dreams to the Magian seers for exposition, and then guiding his actions by the advice they tendered him, the religious zeal of the young Zoroastrian may very naturally have been aroused, and the contest into which he plunged may have been, in his eyes, not so much a national struggle as a crusade against the infidels. It will be found hereafter that religious fervor animated the Persians in most of those wars by which they spread their dominion. We may suspect, therefore, though it must be admitted we cannot prove, that a religious motive was among those which led them to make their first efforts after independence.

According to the account of the struggle which is most circumstantial, and on the whole most probable, the first difficulty which the would-be rebel had to meet and vanquish was that of quitting the Court. Alleging that his father was in weak health, and required his care, he requested leave of absence for a short time; but his petition was refused on the flattering ground that the Great King was too much attached to him to lose sight of him even for a day. A second application, however, made through a favorite eunuch after a certain interval of time, was more successful; Cyrus received permission to absent himself from Court for the next five months; whereupon, with a few attendants, he left Ecbatana by night, and took the road leading to his native country.

The next evening Astyages, enjoying himself as usual over his wine, surrounded by a crowd of his concubines, singing-girls, and dancing-girls, called on one of them for a song. The girl took her lyre and sang as follows: "The lion had the wild boar in his power, but let him depart to his own lair; in his lair he will wax in strength, and will cause the lion a world of toil; till at length, although the weaker, he will overcome the stronger." The words of the song greatly disquieted the king, who had been already made aware that a Chaldaean prophecy designated Cyrus as future king of the Persians. Repenting of the indulgence which he had granted him, Astyages forthwith summoned an officer into his presence, and ordered him to take a body of horsemen, pursue the Persian prince, and bring him back, either alive or dead. The officer obeyed, overtook Cyrus, and announced his errand; upon which Cyrus expressed his perfect willingness to return, but proposed, that, as it was late, they should defer their start till the next day. The Medes consenting, Cyrus feasted them, and succeeded in making them all drunk; then mounting his horse, he rode off at full speed with his attendants, and reached a Persian outpost, where he had arranged with his father that he should find a body of Persian troops. When the Medes had slept off their drunkenness, and found their prisoner gone, they pursued, and again overtaking Cyrus, who was now at the head of an armed force, engaged him. They were, however, defeated with great loss, and forced to retreat, while Cyrus, having beaten them off, made good his escape into Persia.

When Astyages heard what had happened, he was greatly vexed; and, smiting his thigh, he exclaimed, "Ah! fool, thou knewest well that it boots not to heap favors on the vile; yet didst thou suffer thyself to be gulled by smooth words; and so thou hast brought upon thyself this mischief. But even now he shall not get off scot-free." And instantly he sent for his generals, and commanded them to collect his host, and proceed to reduce Persia to obedience. Three thousand chariots, two hundred thousand horse, and a million footmen (!) were soon brought together; and with these Astyages in person invaded the revolted province, and engaged the army which Cyrus and his father Cambyses had collected for defence. This consisted of a hundred chariots, fifty thousand horsemen, and three hundred thousand light-armed foot, who were drawn up in in front of a fortified town near the frontier. The first day's battle was long and bloody, terminating without any decisive advantage to either side; but on the second day Astyages, making skilful use of his superior numbers, gained a great victory. Having detached one hundred thousand men with orders to make a circuit and get into the rear of the town, he renewed the attack; and when the Persians were all intent on the battle in their front, the troops detached fell on the city and took it, almost before its defenders were aware. Cambyses, who commanded in the town, was mortally wounded and fell into the enemy's hands. The army in the field, finding itself between two fires, broke and fled towards the interior, bent on defending Pasargadse, the capital. Meanwhile Astyages, having given Cambyses honorable burial, pressed on in pursuit.

The country had now become rugged and difficult. Between Pasargadse and the place where the two days' battle was fought lay a barrier of lofty hills, only penetrated by a single narrow pass. On either side were two smooth surfaces of rock, while the mountain towered above, lofty and precipitous. The pass was guarded by ten thousand Persians. Recognizing the impossibility of forcing it, Astyages again detached a body of troops, who marched along the foot of the range till they found a place where it could be ascended, when they climbed it and seized the heights directly over the defile. The Persians upon this had to evacuate their strong position, and to retire to a lower range of hills very near to Pasargadge. Here again there was a two days' fight. On the first day all the efforts of the Medes to ascend the range (which, though low, was steep, and covered with thickets of wild olive) were fruitless. Their enemy met them, not merely with the ordinary weapons, but with great masses of stone, which they hurled down with crushing force upon their ascending columns. On the second day, however, the resistance was weaker or less effective Astyages had placed at the foot of the range, below his attacking columns, a body of troops with orders to kill all who refused to ascend, or who, having ascended, attempted to quit the heights and return to the valley. Thus compelled to advance, his men fought with desperation, and drove the Persians before them up the slopes of the hill to its very summit, where the women and children had been placed for the sake of security. There, however, the tide of success turned. The taunts and upbraidings of their mothers and wives restored the courage of the Persians; and, turning upon their foe, they made a sudden furious charge. The Medes, astonished and overborne, were driven headlong down the hill, and fell into such confusion that the Persians slew sixty thousand of them. Still Astyages did not desist from his attack. The authority whom we have been following here to a great extent fails us, and we have only a few scattered notices from which to reconstruct the closing scenes of the war. It would seem from these that Astyages still maintained the offensive, and that there was a fifth battle in the immediate neighborhood of Pasargadse, wherein he was completely defeated by Cyrus, who routed the Median army, and pressing upon them in their flight, took their camp. All the insignia of Median royalty fell into his hands; and, amid the acclamations of his army, he assumed them, and was saluted by his soldiers "King of Media and Persia." Meanwhile Astyages had sought for safety in flight; the greater part of his army had dispersed, and he was left with only a few friends, who still adhered to his fortunes. Could he have reached Ecbatana, he might have greatly prolonged the struggle; but his enemy pressed him close; and, being compelled to an engagement, he not only suffered a complete defeat, but was made prisoner by his fortunate adversary. By this capture the Median monarchy was brought abruptly to an end. Astyages had no son to take his place and continue the struggle. Even had it been otherwise, the capture of the monarch would probably have involved his people's submission. In the East the king is so identified with his kingdom that the possession of the royal person is regarded as conveying to the possessor all regal rights. Cyrus, apparently, had no need even to besiege Ecbatana; the whole Median state, together with its dependencies, at once submitted to him, on learning what had happened. This ready submission was no doubt partly owing to the general recognition of a close connection between Media and Persia, which made the transfer of empire from the one to the other but slightly galling to the subjected power, and a matter of complete indifference to the dependent countries. Except in so far as religion was concerned, the change from one Iranic race to the other would make scarcely a perceptible difference to the subjects of either kingdom. The law of the state would still be "the law of the Medes and Persians." Official employments would be open to the people of both countries. Even the fame and glory of empire would attain, in the minds of men, almost as much to the one nation as the other. If Media descended from her preeminent rank, it was to occupy a station only a little below the highest, and one which left her a very distinct superiority over all the subject races.

If it be asked how Media, in her hour of peril, came to receive no assistance from the great Powers with which she had made such close alliances—Babylonia and Lydia—the answer would seem to be that Lydia was too remote from the scene of strife to lend her effective aid, while circumstances had occurred in Babylonia to detach that state from her and render it unfriendly. The great king, Nebuchadnezzar, had he been on the throne, would undoubtedly have come to the assistance of his brother-in-law, when the fortune of war changed, and it became evident that his crown was in danger. But Nebuchadnezzar had died in B.V. 561, three years before the Persian revolt broke out. His son, Evil-Merodach, who would probably have maintained his father's alliances, had survived him but two years: he had been murdered in B.C. 559 by a brother-in-law, Nergalsharezer or Neriglissar, who ascended the throne in that year and reigned till B.C. 555. This prince was consequently on the throne at the time of Astyages' need. As he had supplanted the house of Nebuchadnezzar, he would naturally be on bad terms with that monarch's Median connections; and we may suppose that he saw with pleasure the fall of a power to which pretenders from the Nebuchadnezzar family would have looked for support and countenance.

In conclusion, a few words may be said on the general character of the Median Empire, and the causes of its early extinction.

The Median Empire was in extent and fertility of territory-equal if not superior to the Assyrian. It stretched from Rhages and the Carmanian desert on the east to the river Halys upon the west, a distance of above twenty degrees, or about 1,300 miles. From north to south it was comparatively narrow, being confined between the Black Sea, the Caucasus, and the Caspian, on the one side, and the Euphrates and Persian Gulf on the other. Its greatest width, which was towards the east, was about nine, and its least, which was towards the west, was about four degrees. Its area was probably not much short of 500,000 square miles. Thus it was as large as Great Britain, France, Spain, and Portugal put together.

In fertility its various parts were very unequal. Portions of both Medias, of Persia, of Armenia, Iberia, and Cappadocia, were rich and productive; but in all these countries there was a large quantity of barren mountain, and in Media Magna and Persia there were tracts of desert. If we estimate the resources of Media from the data furnished by Herodotus in his account of the Persian revenue, and compare them with those of the Assyrian Empire, as indicated by the same document, we shall find reason to conclude, that except during the few years when Egypt was a province of Assyria, the resources of the Third exceeded those of the Second Monarchy.

The weakness of the Empire arose chiefly from its want of organization. Nicolas of Damascus, indeed, in the long passage from which our account of the struggle between Cyrus and Astyages has been taken, represents the Median Empire as divided, like the Persian, into a number of satrapies but there is no real ground for believing that any such organization was practised in Median times, or to doubt that Darius Hystaspis was the originator of the satrapial system. The Median Empire, like the Assyrian, was a congeries of kingdoms, each ruled by its own native prince, as is evident from the case of Persia, where Cambyses was not satrap, but monarch. Such organization as was attempted appears to have been clumsy in the extreme. The Medes (we are told) only claimed direct suzerainty over the nations immediately upon their borders; remoter tribes they placed under these, and looked to them to collect and remit the tribute of the outlying countries. It is doubtful if they called on the subject nations for any contingents of troops. We never hear of their doing so. Probably, like the Assyrians, they made their conquests with armies composed entirely of native soldiers, or of those combined with such forces as were sent to their aid by princes in alliance with them.

The weakness arising from this lack of organization was increased by a corruption of manners, which caused the Medes speedily to decline in energy and warlike spirit. The conquest of a great and luxurious empire by a hardy and simple race is followed, almost of necessity, by a deterioration in the character of the conquerors, who lose the warlike virtues, and too often do not replace them by the less splendid virtues of peace. This tendency, which is fixed in the nature of things, admits of being checked for a while, or rapidly developed, according to the policy and character of the monarchs who happen to occupy the throne. If the original conqueror is succeeded, by two or three ambitious and energetic princes, who engage in important wars and labor to extend their dominions at the expense of their neighbors, it will be some time before the degeneracy becomes marked. If, on the other hand, a prince of a quiet temper, self-indulgent, and studious of ease, come to the throne within a short time of the original conquests, the deterioration will be very rapid. In the present instance it happened that the immediate successor of the first conqueror was of a peaceful disposition, unambitious, and luxurious in his habits. During a reign which lasted at least thirty-five years he abstained almost wholly from military enterprises; and thus an entire generation of Medes grew up without seeing actual service, which alone makes the soldier. At the same time there was a general softening of manners. The luxury of the Court corrupted the nobles, who from hardy mountain chieftains, simple if not even savage in their dress and mode of life, became polite courtiers, magnificent in their apparel, choice in their diet, and averse to all unnecessary exertion. The example of the upper classes would tell on the lower, though not perhaps to any very large extent. The ordinary Mede, no doubt, lost something of his old daring and savagery; from disuse he became inexpert in the management of arms; and he was thus no longer greatly to be dreaded as a soldier. But he was really not very much less brave, nor less capable of bearing hardships, than before; and it only required a few years of training to enable him to recover himself and to be once more as good a soldier as any in Asia.

But in the affairs of nations, as in those of men, negligence often proves fatal before it can be repaired. Cyrus saw his opportunity, pressed his advantage, and established the supremacy of his nation, before the unhappy effects of Astyages' peace policy could be removed. He knew that his own Persians possessed the military spirit in its fullest vigor; he felt that he himself had all the qualities of a successful loader; he may have had faith in his cause, which, he would view as the cause of Ormazd against Ahriman, of pure Religion against a corrupt and debasing nature-worship. His revolt was sudden, unexpected, and well-timed. He waited till Astyages was advanced in years, and so disqualified for command; till the veterans of Cyaxares were almost all in their graves; and till the Babylonian throne was occupied by a king who was not likely to afford Astyages any aid. Ho may not at first have aspired to do more than establish the independence of his own country. But when the opportunity of effecting a transfer of empire offered itself, he seized it promptly; rapidly repeating his blows, and allowing his enemy no time to recover and renew the struggle. The substitution of Persia for Media as the ruling power in Western Asia was due less to general causes than to the personal character of two men. Had

Astyages been a prince of ordinary vigor, the military training of the Medes would have been kept up; and in that case they might easily have hold their own against all comers. Had their training been kept up, or had Cyrus possessed no more than ordinary ambition and ability, either he would not have thought of revolting, or he would have revolted unsuccessfully. The fall of the Median Empire was due immediately to the genius of the Persian Prince; but its ruin was prepared, and its destruction was really caused, by the shortsightedness of the Median monarch.

www.ingramcontent.com/pod-product-compliance
Lightning Source LLC
Chambersburg PA
CBHW060146050426
42448CB00010B/2321